The
Encourage**MINT**

A wealth of daily inspiration,
encouraging you to become
who God says You Are -- In Him.

Michael E. Evans

ARMOUR OF LIGHT
P U B L I S H I N G
Chapel Hill, North Carolina

Published in the United States of America by
Armour of Light Publishing
P.O. Box 778
Chapel Hill, North Carolina 27514

Visit us at: www.theencouragemint.com
            www.armouroflight.org

Design by Michael E. Evans
UR Coin design by Alex Radin: www.truthillustrations.com

Paperback Edition: ISBN 0 - 9620604 - 2 - 9
Hard Cover Edition: ISBN 0 - 9620604 - 3 - 7

Library of Congress Control Number 2004098253

First Edition

All scriptures quoted from the Authorized King James Version unless otherwise noted.

10 9 8 7 6 5 4 3 2

To those who have failed.

To those who have succeeded
at something other than that which was intended.

To those who have learned to be content, but long to be satisfied.

"*You are more than you have become.*"

DISNEY'S -- The Lion King

You Are (UR) -- correct.

ACKNOWLEDGEMENTS *(ROMANS 1:8-12)*

If you are thinking that I could not have possibly written this book by myself, you are correct. God has been connecting me with the right people all my life. The love, patience, faithfulness, and influence of these exceptional souls have made, not only this book, but my life possible. Many of them are mentioned in the text, but it would take another book, altogether, to mention everyone and thank them properly, so I'll just let you in on some highlights. They know the real story.

First Chance: Thanks mom and dad for making us go to church. Thanks Kurt for rededicating your life to Christ and praying for my salvation. Thanks Mike & Norma for all your giving and never giving up on me. You put the "bite" in my bark. Thanks Dr. John Rennick for asking such an obvious question: *"Why not raise heaven?"* Thanks Brian for making us read "Our Daily Bread." Thanks Bruce for making it clear that I needed to be saved. Thanks Cheryl for preaching: *"Time Now To Serve The Lord."* Thanks Angie for letting me tag along with you and Bruce, feeding me almost everyday and taking me to Dr. Vanderbilt's to get filled with the Holy Spirit. Thanks James *(looking on from that great cloud of witnesses)* for inviting me to Mount Zion. Thanks Pastor Fozard for being my pastor for twenty-two years. Thanks Dr. Fletcher for moving to America, sleeping in Bruce & Angie's back bedroom, teaching us songs and telling us about fasting and miracles. Thanks Pastor Gool for encouraging me to "run" with my calling. Thanks Verla for prophesying my "Proverbial" move to Chapel Hill.

For almost thirteen years, I had the marvelous privilege of pastoring The Lord's Church of Chapel Hill, NC and starting other TLC's in four states. My sincerest apologies to all the saints and ministry gifts that I disappointed. Thank you for your prayers. Thank you for holding true to your convictions even though, in some cases, I still find myself on the wrong end of them. I look forward to our glorious reunion.

Second Chance: Thanks Craig, Stephanie & Jordan, for giving me someplace to go. Thanks Pastor Bobby & Jane Causey and the entire Eastside Fellowship family for loving us without even blinking. Thanks again Kurt for challenging me to rely on God's mercy and grace. Thanks Bob & Carol Champion for really believing that the gifts and callings of God are without repentance. Thanks Cliff for putting me on the air. Thanks Pastor Easley for encouraging me to preach again. Thanks Carol for putting me to work and allowing God to use you to sustain us. Thanks Mount Zion *(Durham, Rocky Mount & Henderson)* for forgiving. Thanks Pastor Philip Miles and the saints at Christ Community Church for welcoming me back. Thanks Pastor Chip Judd for helping us talk it out. Thanks Ms. Atwater for being faithful. Thanks Pastor Subash Cherion and all the saints at Highland Church for staying connected. Thanks Will for being a patient teacher, listener, editor, and friend. And last but definitely not least, thanks Gloria for helping me.

TABLE OF CONTENTS

iv Acknowledgements
ix Foreword
x Introduction
xii Tips

January
1 as He is in this world
2 walking in eternity
3 a new creature
4 still here
5 smarter than you know
6 authentic
7 the light of the world
8 more than a conqueror
9 going to rejoice and be glad
10 going to be the battle
11 dust
12 here
13 well represented
14 more than you have become
15 oh yes you are!
16 armed with a dream
17 the greatest
18 a dreamer
19 followers of God
20 blessed
21 extremely valuable
22 a curious kind of confident
23 out of sight
24 powerful
25 the apple of God's eye
26 free
27 going to get your chance
28 called to be a saint
29 a living soul (1)
30 a living soul (2)
31 a living soul (3)

February
1 not your own
2 the whether man
3 redeemed
4 taking a turn for the better
5 more excellent than your neighbor
6 just 17 inches from "there"
7 light in the Lord
8 fulfilling the law of God (1)
9 fulfilling the law of God (2)
10 fulfilling the law of God (3)
11 sitting pretty
12 fulfilling the law of God (4)

13 fulfilling the law of God (5)
14 loved (Valentine)
15 sitting on a gold mine
16 fulfilling the law of God (6)
17 fulfilling the law of God (7)
18 fulfilling the law of God (8)
19 fulfilling the law of God (9)
20 a keeper
21 nobody's fool
22 fulfilling the law of God (10)
23 bone of his bone...
24 selfish
25 jealous
26 a witness
27 narrow minded
28 surrounded
29 taking a leap of faith

March
1 married / subject to Christ
2 forgetting something
3 going where God wants you to
4 covered
5 the righteousness of God
6 a human being
7 working with the best
8 going through hell
9 being followed
10 strong in the Lord
11 inconsiderate
12 a child of God
13 the salt of the earth
14 highly favored
15 F.R.E.E.
16 a ready writer
17 a disciple whom Jesus loves
18 absolutely alive
19 confused
20 worshipping His Majesty
21 just perfect
22 an ambassador
23 admitted
24 all in the family
25 between a rock and a hard place
26 second
27 crucified with Christ
28 sanctified
29 well taken care of
30 well equipped to handle fear
31 Abraham's seed

TABLE OF CONTENTS

April
1   nobody's fool
2   anointed
3   God's workmanship
4   delightful
5   born again
6   holding the truth
7   your brother's keeper (1)
8   your brother's keeper (2)
9   worthy
10 a good soldier
11 a natural
12 God's people
13 worthy of your meat
14 justified
15 a taxpayer
16 in for a surprise
17 being talked about
18 beyond words
19 too quick to judge
20 a true worshipper
21 following a pattern
22 a troublemaker
23 not matching your background
24 strong
25 in Christ
26 changing
27 going to see the King
28 one of many sons
29 always going to win
30 not to fear

May
1   standing in the gap
2   de branch
3   welcomed
4   lacking one thing
5   coming in loud and clear
6   full of it
7   not going to believe it
8   holy
9   baptized into one body
10 approved
11 in hot pursuit
12 being watched
13 standing on holy ground
14 a winner (1)
15 a winner (2)
16 a winner (3)
17 a winner (4)
18 a winner (5)

19 a winner (6)
20 promised protection
21 getting through
22 my wife
23 not alone
24 not ashamed
25 a lively stone
26 a breath of fresh air
27 saying something
28 not a quitter
29 mine
30 Christ's
31 the temple of God

June
1   challenged to choose
2   charged with a choice
3   drawing closer to your goal
4   in need of a cause
5   selected and highlighted
6   proof positive
7   someone's joy and crown
8   precious
9   seeing 'em like you call 'em
10 safe
11 my husband
12 not seeing things
13 not hearing things
14 flying a new flag
15 wise
16 renewed day by day
17 fearfully and wonderfully made
18 well staffed
19 in need of patience
20 what you are...
21 loaded
22 incomparable
23 a workman
24 selling yourself cheap
25 the voice of victory
26 a whoso(ever)
27 going to the other side
28 called to be...
29 beautiful
30 looking quite becoming

July
1   almost home
2   loud, delirious & redundant
3   an insider
4   unentangled

TABLE OF CONTENTS

July
5 a tree planted by the waters
6 a blessing
7 coming out
8 going through
9 going to fall
10 coming in
11 surrounded by miracles
12 behind that preposition
13 on God's mind
14 wiser than your enemies
15 resting
16 blessed indeed
17 converted
18 tongue-tied
19 on fire
20 allowed one giant step
21 sealed
22 kept by the power of God
23 expecting
24 engaged
25 clean
26 not ignorant
27 doing...
28 called and chosen and faithful
29 alive
30 on the road to perfection
31 cursed with a curse

August
1 temperate in all things
2 going to die
3 built up
4 illuminated
5 a walking word
6 following your confession
7 just getting started
8 fighting for something grand
9 a contender
10 a triple threat
11 a triple threat (soul)
12 a triple threat (spirit)
13 a triple threat (body)
14 a triple threat
15 a man after God's own heart
16 prepared for takeoff
17 not a sinner
18 a forecaster
19 enriched

20 called to obedience
21 privileged
22 not what you used to be
23 too sensitive
24 it
25 the word made flesh
26 adopted
27 asking amiss
28 what you think you are
29 out of order
30 in the kingdom for such a time as this
31 my friend

September
1 an EncourageMINT
2 an EncourageMINT
3 an EncourageMINT
4 an EncourageMINT
5 declaring your worth
6 going to try again
7 going down
8 holding things up
9 the head and not the tail
10 framing your world
11 free from terror
12 doing well
13 going to have a good day
14 special
15 ministers of reconciliation
16 in an impossible situation
17 sin repellent
18 working out
19 seeking the kingdom
20 waiting patiently
21 singing a new song
22 Christ's prisoner
23 running out of time
24 about your Father's business
25 being used
26 a beloved child...
27 making the most of today
28 the sheep of His hand
29 before Abraham
30 runnin' and ain't nothin' at ya

October
1 naked
2 not dropping the ball
3 not guilty

TABLE OF CONTENTS

4   out of focus
5   changing
6   a prayer-making, prison breaker
7   going to find what you are looking for
8   somebody
9   made in God's image
10 not God
11 being talked about
12 getting a second chance
13 in need of patience
14 outnumbered
15 in labor
16 facing a deadline
17 what you are AND...
18 why
19 in over your head
20 in over your head
21 in over your head
22 in over your head
23 in over your head
24 granted your request
25 abiding under the shadow...
26 content
27 eligible for Witness Protection
28 the spitting image of your Father
29 getting hungry
30 profitable
31 the undead

November
1   all saints
2   God's elect
3   partaking of the divine nature
4   profitable for ministry
5   in for a taste treat
6   healed
7   the sheep of His hand
8   as a watered garden
9   chosen
10 your ways
11 a fish out of water
12 a fish out of water
13 a fish out of water
14 expected
15 a friend
16 a comforter
17 older than Methuselah
18 We *is* one
19 a slice of baloney

20 moving
21 pregnant
22 regaining a lot
23 seen and heard of God
24 getting fat
25 full
26 working your buts off
27 a child of promise
28 causing others to worship
29 choosing your children
30 changing your children

December
1   charging your children
2   chauffering your children
3   cheering your children
4   cheating your children
5   a chosen child
6   challenging your children
7   trees of righteousness
8   renovating
9   at liberty to flee
10 stretching the truth
11 working
12 death defiant
13 God's delight
14 called to lend
15 not a thief
16 making a living
17 a success
18 out of luck
19 a wise fool
20 flying solo
21 a guiding light
22 God's gift
23 invited to dinner
24 the reason for the season
25 the Christ...
26 in the beginning
27 in the beginning
28 in the beginning
29 in the beginning
30 breathing
31 called to repentance

219 Praise for the EncourageMINT
222 Making A Mint
223 Thanks...You Are greatly appreciated
223 About The Author
224 An Encouraging Prayer

"Freedom requires faith."

FOREWORD

S o many people go through life without realizing their full potential. Because we are weighed down by life's baggage - sin, guilt, disappointment, addiction, unforgiveness and shame - we spend most of our energy balancing that crushing load. Tragically, many people simply collapse under the weight.

Yet the Bible says Jesus provided a way for us to find freedom and fulfillment. He can lift our burden, deliver us from shame, break the power of sin and grant us the grace to live a life of joy and blessing. He made this possible through the amazing miracle of His death and resurrection. Yet we cannot appropriate the blessings and benefits of that miracle until we decide to believe. Freedom requires faith.

And how do we come to the point that we truly believe? That can happen only through the process of reading God's Word and allowing the power of His promises to change our minds. Romans 12:2, in fact, commands us to "renew" our minds with His Word:

> *"And do not be conformed to this world, but be transformed by the renewing of your mind, so that you may prove what the will of God is, that which is good and acceptable and perfect"* (NASB).

This book is a simple but powerful tool to help you transform your thinking. Author Michael E. Evans knows from his own personal experience that if you will saturate your thoughts with the promises of God and learn to daily meditate on the Bible's liberating truths, your view of life will change.

God's Word will wash you clean from guilt, break your bad habits, change your negative self-image and free you from the limitations that have been imposed on you by your own inadequacy or by the failures and disappointments of life.

I challenge you to follow this daily study of God's Word and allow these words to soak deeply into every crevice of your mind. The power of the Holy Spirit will give you a level of freedom you have never known and launch you out into a new and exciting spiritual adventure.

J. Lee Grady, Editor
Charisma Magazine

This devotional was born of a simple revelation. I am what God, the great I AM, says I am -- no matter what I have become.

INTRODUCTION

On January 1, 2003 I began to send daily e-mails that I hoped would encourage a small list of friends and associates. These e-mails, though similar to some business e-mails and web work I had experimented with earlier, were, also, very different. My goal from the beginning was to create a devotional that I would put in print form. For years, I have been blessed by and amazed at the agelessness of the writings of Oswald Chambers *(My Utmost For His Highest)* and dreamed that maybe my writings might be half as inspiring.

One of my favorite authors, Chinua Achebe, says that there must be three reasons for writing. First you must have an overpowering urge to tell a story. Second you must have intimations that the story waiting to come out is unique. And finally you must consider the project worth the considerable trouble *(he calls it the terms of imprisonment)* you will have to endure to bring it to fruition.

Well, I can't think of anything that I have ever wanted to do more. Writing these daily e-mails has been a pure expression of my calling. I believe they are tied to my own course, helping people to Find, Follow and Finish their courses in life.

Ten years prior to starting The EncourageMINT, I made a decision that changed my life. I remember where I was and what I was doing when I made it. Terrible choices and selfish habits had contributed to the ruin of my marriage, and I remember getting tired of "waiting on God" to fix it. It seems foolish *(pronounced: suicidal)* now, but then I thought, *"I'll fix this myself."*

I committed adultery. I deceived my family, my church, and my friends. I dishonored my calling and gave great occasion for the enemies of God to blaspheme. Words cannot describe how my life changed after I *"fixed"* things. Things kept going, business as usual, for a long while. But as all disconnected branches do, I ultimately began to wither and die. And on March 27, 1997, the Saturday before Easter, I walked out of my home, my marriage, my ministry and my life.

Like Jonah's, my life went down from there. I remember hesitating when people asked me my name. I had been Pastor Evans for so long, I didn't know what to call myself. When they asked what I did for a living, the only thing I could do was laugh. I started writing again. It became an outlet -- a kind of catharsis. And that eventually brought me to The EncourageMINT.

In the fall of 2002, I was reading John 8:58 where Jesus said *"before Abraham was I AM."* That's when God said: *"You can replace Abraham's name with anything."*

Immediately, the Holy Spirit began to bring scriptures to my remembrance. Inwardly I shouted, *"As He is, so am I in this world."* (1 John 4:17)

BEFORE ANYTHING WAS, I AM...

I remembered John Zabawski quoting The Lion King in a sermon: *"Simba. You are more than you have become."* I had repented, and I knew I was forgiven, but suddenly, I was on a mission to stop being what I had become and become what God says I am. It was at that point my inconsistent, disconnected, linear life, got rejoined to the unbroken circle of God's love and I stepped back into the infinite eternal. It was at that point Jesus circumvented my circumstances.

It seems that the daily e-mails have blessed many people. Return e-mails, letters, cards, phone calls and even faxes have often surprised us. People comment on the timeliness of the messages. Some forward them to their lists so that we have no idea how many people are reading them. I know that when I miss a day or two, I hear about it. Hits to the web site are increasing daily and our e-mail list is growing. But I believe the greatest benefit has been to me, personally. The EncourageMINT has been a source of hope. An anchor. A beacon. A constant reminder of God's expectation. (Jeremiah 29:11) Truly, His gifts and callings are without repentance.

"Jabez was more honorable than his brethren" long before his mother labeled him sorrowful. The younger son (the prodigal), having left home and father, *"came to himself."* And for the first time in years, I woke up recently, prompted by the Holy Spirit to read the story of Samson. Judges 13:7 says: *"...the child shall be a Nazarite to God from the womb to the day of his death."* We all know Samson made some terrible choices. But the declaration of God held true.

Truly, Jesus is the author and finisher of our faith. It is God that works in us both to will and to do of His good pleasure. And we can be confident of this very thing, that He which has begun a good work in us will perform it until the day of Jesus Christ.

Jabez was granted his request and the younger son made it home. And though Samson died reclaiming his heritage, the prophecy of God came to pass. Believe me, I am in no hurry to die. There are some things I have yet to do. There is some good work that God has yet to perform in me. *"Before divorce was, I am..."* called to preach the gospel and encourage you to become who God says you are.

This book is the manifesto of an all-out effort to call those things which be not, as though they were. The great I AM wants us to believe that He is, so that we can stop being what we have become, and become who We Are -- In Him.

Michael E. Evans
Charleston, SC
October 11, 2004

TIPS *(Get the most out of The EncourageMINT)*

Read It:
> *Paul instructed Timothy to "give attendance to reading." Electronics notwithstanding, there is an imprint that is made on our hearts and minds when we read. The noble Christians of Berea received the word gladly; then they went home and "searched the scriptures" to see if what they heard was true. (1 Timothy 4:13 / Acts 17:10,11)*

Teach It:
> *Sunday School & Bible Studies -- One of the best ways to strengthen your grasp of a concept is to make the commitment to share it with others. Real knowledge is reproductive. (2 Timothy 2:22-26)*

Preach It:
> *We suggest hosting a **Second Chance Series**. The EncourageMINT is really designed to give people a glimpse of who they are so that they can recover from what they have become. Bold proclamation of these eternal truths, <u>in concord with practical application</u>, can transform broken lives. (Mark 16:15-20 / Romans 10:13-17) For more information, contact us at: **www.theencouragemint.com***

Share It:
> *Since we began sending these nuggets as e-mails, people have been forwarding them to friends & loved ones. Thank you for buying the book, so that we can carry on our ministry, but please share it with others. Better yet, buy additional copies for your friends and family. (2 Corinthians 8:1-5)*

Encourage Others: *(Especially those who have failed.)*
> *Again, The EncourageMINT is really designed to give people a glimpse of who they are so that they can recover from what they have become. Bold proclamation of these eternal truths can transform broken lives. (Isaiah 41:6-8)*

One Click Inspiration:
> *This devotional began as a daily e-mail to a small list of friends. I threatened to stop sending them once and discovered, the hard way, that people love the convenience of "one click inspiration." Send us your e-mail address and get on the list. Or hit us on the web at:* **www.theencouragemint.com** *email:* **daily@theencouragemint.com**

You Are (UR) -- as He is in this world.

(1 JOHN 4:17) JANUARY 1

He that cometh to God must believe that He is. (Hebrews 11:6) This is the first fundamental of faith. This is not mere mental assent. We do more than agree that there is a God. We are dependent upon His existence. For by Him all things consist. (Colossians 1:15-17)

Thomas Aquinas described God in the thirteenth century as: *"the only being whose essence is Existence, all other beings being contingent on God, who is Being (or Is-ness) itself."* From the beginning, His design was to make us in His image and after His likeness.

> *"God created man in his own image,*
> *in the image of God created he him;*
> *male and female created he them."*
> **Genesis 1:27**

God, being the author and the finisher of our faith, now encourages us to remind you of what He made. To direct you to revisit who you are -- in Him. To remind you of what you really look like, as it were.

Each passage in this devotional starts with **You Are (UR)**, because it is you who needs encouragement. But the you that we refer to is not the you that you now see. It is not the you that most of us are familiar with. It is not the you that you have become. The you that we begin each passage with is the you that He envisions. And like Him, we call those things which be not, as though they were. (Romans 4:17)

Surely we have forgotten what manner of men we are. We have beheld ourselves in a glass and gone our way. But now we look into the perfect law of liberty and continue therein. And we will not just look. We will not just hear. We will do. We will be doers of the work and be blessed in our deed. (James 1:22-25) We are determined to become and encourage you to become **as He is in this world**.

You Are (UR) -- walking in eternity.

JANUARY 2 *(JOHN 3:16)*

1. Your birthday began your natural life -- a finite line, filled with ups and downs, destined to end in death. **2.** But the everlasting Father knew you before you were formed in your mother's womb and ordained you to His chosen life. **3.** Adam sold you into sin -- separating you from God for a season. **4.** But Jesus, the Son of God, descended from heaven to break the curse of sin and reconnect you to the Father. **5.** Now your sins are blotted out and and you are, once again, walking in eternity.

W hat you just read is a nugget -- valuable currency -- coinage from a brand new mint -- The EncourageMINT.

The Encourage**MINT** is a storehouse whose sole purpose is to process ore. *(Be what it says or be what others say about you. It's your choice.)*

This ore is **Y-O-U**ranium. The force of life. It is the substance worlds are made of. (Heb 12:1-6) It is the word of God.

When you open it everyday, it will radiate. But don't worry, it will only affect you if you agree with it -- believe it -- say it -- confess it -- prophesy with it. (1 Samuel 10:6)

Remember:
It will always say what **You (UR) Are**. Now it's up to you to make it personal and say I AM. That's not just sentence structure. That's the name, the very presence, of God. (Ex. 3:13,14) **YH--WH** or Yahweh. Breathe in and shout it out. He IS the breath of life. (Psalm 150:6)

Your confident confession will make you a new creature (2 Cor. 5:17). It will cause you to come to yourself and rise up. (Lk. 15:11-32 {17}) You are fearfully and wonderfully made and you will praise the God that made you when your soul knows that right well.

You Are (UR) -- a new creature.

(2 CORINTHIANS 5:17) JANUARY 3

Bullfrogs and Butterflies, they've both been born again. The children used to sing that song to illustrate the metamorphosis that is the new birth. Truly, a transformation is taking place in all of us who are in Christ.

Because this change is at the heart of our christian experience, let's make sure we understand what is happening. 2 Corinthians 5:17 begins with the word, *"Therefore."* Whenever you see *"therefore"* in your Bible, you need to back up and see what it's there for. Verses 14-16 remind us that Christ died for us. They charge us that this supreme act of love demands a specific reaction -- that we ought no longer live unto ourselves, but unto Him which died for us and rose again. Verse 16 charges us to *"know...no man after the flesh."* That includes our *"old man"* and that's where the newness kicks in.

Paul begs us, in Romans 12, *"by the mercies of God,"* to present our bodies *"a living sacrifice."* Consider his plea. Everything that has happened to you in this life -- good or bad -- Paul asks you to sacrifice it. Offer it up willingly, expecting a heavenly return. He asks that you *"count it all...loss,"* as he did, (Philippians 3:1-14) that you might *"win Christ."*

So what do we win? We win the right to begin again. We win the chance to be new. When Samuel anointed Saul king in 1 Samuel 10, he told him three things about his life. **First** -- The donkeys he was looking for had been found. *(God had taken care of his past.)* **Second** -- He would soon meet men with food and drink. *(God would take care of his "daily bread.")* **Third** -- He would meet musical prophets coming down from the *"high place"* and they would *"prophesy."*

Samuel told Saul that the Spirit of the Lord would come upon him and instructed him to *"prophesy with them."* Samuel prophesied that Saul would then *"be turned into another man."*

Your past is forgiven. *"Old things are passed away."* God will meet your every need. You will have what you need today. And if you will agree with the testimony of Jesus -- *"the spirit of prophecy"* -- that dwells in you, (Revelation 19:10) you, too, will be turned into another man. You will discover the transformed you. You are a new creature in Christ Jesus.

You Are (UR) -- still here.

JANUARY 4 *(1 THESSALONIANS 4:17)*

You are the seal of God's faithfulness. You are proof that He will never leave us. You are evidence of his mercy and long-suffering. You are the product of His love.

Try though you may, you can't remember anyone He has forgotten. And there is no redeeming those He has forsaken. Even Balaam knew -- *"I cannot go beyond the word of the Lord my God, to do less or more."* (Numbers 22:12-18) He knew it because God had told him, *"...thou shalt not curse the people: for they are blessed."*

You are the people. You are blessed. And you are still here.

You Are (UR) -- smarter than you know.

JANUARY 5 *(PSALM 139:1-6)*

Sound like an oxymoron? It is not. Consider these facts. We know in part, but one day we will know as we are known. (1 Corinthians 13:12) That limited knowledge is due to the frailties of the flesh. Put simply, unless you are Albert Einstein or Jimmy Neutron, your brain is not but so big and you don't use but 10 to 13% of it.

That notwithstanding, we have the mind of Christ. (1 Corinthians 2:16) And regardless of the size of our frontal lobes, attention focused on obedience to the revealed will/word of God gives us instant access to the wisdom of the ages. (Psalm 119:97-104/Proverbs 1:7/Ecclesiastes 12:12&13/James 1:16-25) You are smarter than you know.

You Are (UR) -- authentic.

(MATTHEW 7:28,29) JANUARY 6

The scribes and the pharisees drudged through their working lives, doing what they "had to do." They had become religious professionals, working to make money. The glory had departed and they hadn't heard from God in over four hundred years. (Malachi 2:8,9) Lots of people live uninspired lives, working just to make money. But unless you're employed in a mint, that attitude makes you little more than a counterfeiter -- or worse -- a counterfeit.

Make no mistake, money is important. Solomon said it *"answereth all things."* (Ecclesiastes 10:19) But there is work that you *"must do."* (Exodus 18:20) There is a vocation that you are called to. (Ephesians 4:1) There are good works that God is expecting you to walk in. (Ephesians 2:8-10) And we are instructed to *"work out"* our own salvation with *"fear and trembling."* (Philippians 2:12,13)

In all these things, we manifest God's authorized design for our lives. We are *"sent,"* as Paul said to the Romans concerning they who preach the gospel. (Romans 10:13-17) You are not a counterfeit. You are authentic.

You Are (UR) -- the light of the world.

(MATTHEW 5:14-16) JANUARY 7

Gotta stay focused. If your eye is single, your whole body will be full of light. (Matthew 6:22/Proverbs 20:27/Romans 8:16) But when you get double (evil) minded, (James 1:8) the world is left to follow a dark light. (Matthew 6:23) And we all know that where there is no vision, the people perish. (Proverbs 29:18)

Here's a thought: Isn't it odd that night vision goggles cause things to appear green and it's usually the pursuit of green (money) that causes men to be double minded.? (Matthew 6:24 & 1 Timothy 6:10)

You Are (UR) -- more than a conqueror.

JANUARY 8 *(ROMANS 8:37)*

Conquerors win battles, defeat people, overthrow cities and kingdoms. They often leave an angry wake of death and destruction. But you -- you impact the world. Your victories uplift the downtrodden and leave the defeated in victory. Can't see it? Neither could the servant of Elisha. (2 Kings 6:8-23)

When he saw the hills of Dothan covered with Syrian garrisons looking to capture his master, Elisha's servant inquired nervously: *"Alas Master, how shall we do?"* Elisha replied: *"Fear not: for they that be with us are more than they that be with them."* Elisha knew that his servant couldn't see it, so he prayed. *"Lord, I pray thee, open his eyes, that he may see."*

The mountain was full of fiery horses and chariots, protecting the man of God. Elisha prayed further that the Lord would smite his enemies with blindness, and he led them, groping in darkness, to Samaria. When their eyes were opened, they saw that all who sought to capture Elisha were now captives themselves. (Ephesians 4:8)

The king of Israel wanted to kill them. Like James and John of Jesus' company (Luke 9:51-56) or the disciples of Acts 1:4-8. Like so many believers, full of zeal without knowledge, seeking *"the wealth of the wicked"* today. He sought to use this powerful opportunity to satisfy the longings of his flesh.

But Elijah knew what Spirit he was of. He knew that vengeance is the Lord's. (Hebrews 10:30) He fed his enemies and sent them safely home and they troubled him no more. Conquerors seek mere advantage and gain. You seek the souls of men. You know that greater is He that is in you than he that is in the world. (1 John 4:4) You know that Godliness with contentment is great gain. (1 Timothy 6:6) You are more than a conqueror.

You Are (UR) -- going to rejoice and be glad TODAY!

(PSALM 118:24) JANUARY 9

I know you are, because I know you know that TODAY is the only day you have. Trite but true: Yesterday is gone and tomorrow is not promised.

NOW is the accepted time; behold, NOW is the day of salvation. (2 Corinthians 6:2) TODAY you are going to add some substance to the things you are hoping for and some evidence to the things you desire but have yet to see. You are going to exercise some NOW faith -- TODAY! (Hebrews 11:1)

You Are (UR) -- going to be the battle.

(1 SAMUEL 17:17-30) JANUARY 10

Young David left the sheep he tended with a keeper and went to take food to his brothers in the army, as his father instructed. When he arrived, he found King Saul and the armies of Israel hiding behind rocks -- trembling at the accusations of Goliath, the giant of the Philistines. When David inquired about the arrangements for Goliath's destruction, David's older brother, Eliab accused him of negligence, pride and naughtiness of heart. (see vs.28)

Unfortunately, Eliab made one huge mistake. He thought David was a timid spectator like him. But David didn't come to *see* the battle. David came to *be* the battle. **Say it out loud!** I didn't come to watch the world happen around me. I will not neglect my gift. I humble myself in the sight of the Lord. I will go where He tells me to and do what He asks me to do. My heart is pure and undivided. I am here to play my part. I didn't come to see the battle. I am going to be the battle!

You Are (UR) -- dust.

JANUARY 11 *(PSALM 103:13,14)*

That's not a put down. That's a relief. It is a gentle reminder to lighten up. We forget we are dust. (Genesis 2:7) I mean really: Dust doing calculus? Dust driving a luxury sedan? Dust reading e-mail? It's easy to forget. Consequently, we've got unattainable expectations and suffer insufferable condemnation. But God remembers and has mercy. Dust rides the wind. So relax and enjoy the trip.

You Are (UR) -- here.

JANUARY 12 *(PHILIPPIANS 4:10,11)*

There are probably times when you wonder where *'here'* is, or perhaps, how you got *'here'*. Most of us will spend our lives trying desperately to get from *'here'* to *'there'*. *(Wherever 'there' is.)* But one thing is certain. If/When you ever get *'there'*, you will have gotten *'there'* from *'here'*. Confusing? Believe me -- It can get nauseating.

You may find it comforting to look for the X or the red dot -- you know -- like the one on the mall directory. *(Distinction being, yours would be made of wood and covered with blood. See Colossians 1:9-29 especially vss 20,21 & 28)*

Ironically, the very first question God ever asked a man (Adam) was: 'Where are you?' He's been finding us lost ever since. (Luke 19:10) God repositioned the first Adam with a red dot -- the bloody hide of a freshly slain animal. (Hebrews 9:22) He prepositioned *(Before ordained where we should always be relative to everything)* us through the last Adam -- Jesus. HE *(His shed blood)* IS our red dot and His cross marks THE (John 14:6) spot. In Him is where you always want to be. (Philippians 3:1-11 especially vs 9)

You Are (UR) -- well represented.

(1 John 2:1,2) JANUARY 13

Jesus, your advocate, is seated on the right hand of the Father, continually making intercession for you. (Hebrews 7:25) The Holy Spirit is interceding also, helping your infirmities. (Romans 8:26-28) The eyes of the Lord are running *(The devil is walking about seeking whom he may devour. 1 Peter 5:8)* to and fro throughout the whole earth on your behalf. (2 Chronicles 16:9) The angels are sent specifically to minister for you. (Hebrews 1:13,14)

And while you are being cheered on by a great cloud of witnesses, (Hebrews 12:1,2) even your difficulties are prepared to work for you. (2 Corinthians 4:15-18) Actually, all things are for your sake, that the abundant grace might through the thanksgiving of many redound to the glory of God. (2 Corinthians 4:15)

Bottom line -- There are a whole lot more folk on your side than there will ever be to resist you. (2 Kings 6:15-17) That notwithstanding, the one thing that will not only stop them, but actually turn them against you -- is pride. (James 4:6-10) So relax. Stop trying to do it yourself. You are well represented.

You Are (UR) -- more than you have become.

(Romans 4:17) JANUARY 14

If you have children, you may recognize this as a message from The Lion King rather than the King of kings. But just because it's not in the Bible, doesn't mean it's un-biblical. Abraham, Moses, Saul, David, Jabez, Gideon, and a host of others suffered from unrealized potential and had to be convinced by God that there was more to them than they had yet seen. From name changes to a barrage of miracles, He showed each of them that He is the God who calls those things which be not as though they were.

You Are (UR) -- oh yes you are!

JANUARY 15 *(ECCLESIASTES 5:3)*

As we celebrate the birthday of Dr. Martin Luther King, Jr., let's remember that what he had was a dream. A glorious dream it was, but it was still just a dream. Dr. King understood that dreams come by the multitude of business, and he used the force of his presence to *"real-eyes"* his dream.

Remember: The first principle of faith is: *"He that cometh to God must believe that he is, and that he is a rewarder of them that diligently seek him."* Who is going to make Dr. King's dream come true? And perhaps more importantly: Who is going to make your dreams come true? You are. Oh yes you are!

You Are (UR) -- armed with a dream.

JANUARY 16 *(GENESIS 37-48)*

Dr. Martin Luther King, Jr. believed in nonviolent civil disobedience. Some considered him a weak pacifist who put himself and others in harm's way. Compared to the militant railings and glistening hardware of contemporaries like Malcolm X and the Nation of Islam or Eldridge Cleaver's Black Panther Party, Dr. King's marches probably seemed a bit benign. But make no mistake: Dr. Martin Luther King, Jr. was well armed. He was A-R-M-E-D with a D-R-E-A-M.

Warning: *(Don't try this at home. We are professionals. Years of Scrabble, Perquackey, Boggle, and Crossword Puzzles just make the letters dance;-)*

Dr. Martin Luther King, Jr. was armed with a vision of what could be and the willing ability to articulate that to the masses. Dr. King proved that neither dogs, water hoses, jail cells, nor guns, can stop one who dares to say what he sees before seeing what he says. You are armed with a dream.

You Are (UR) -- the greatest.

(LUKE 9:46-48) JANUARY 17

I know that Muhamad Ali claimed that title for himself, and it is only fitting that this insight be shared on his birthday. But I think, even the champ realized that his greatness was disputeable outside the boxing ring.

Others, including Ali, would proclaim that God is great. And there is no disputing that. He Is. But Jesus declared that *"he that is least among you,"* the servant, *"the same shall be great."* In this we can all share that great proclamation, *"I am the greatest!"* because we are the servants of all.

You Are (UR) -- a dreamer.

(GENESIS 37-50) JANUARY 18

The story of Joseph is far too vast to cover in a paragraph. But there is one theme that runs throughout his life. He was a dreamer.

Joseph was a dreamer in his father's house. He may have been a bit arrogant in his youth, but how proud would we have been in our coat of many colors, knowing in our hearts that God would use us for great and mighty things? That notwithstanding, *"Pride goes before destruction, and a haughty spirit before a fall."* (Proverbs 16:18) And fall, Joseph did. His brothers took his coat and left him for dead. But Joseph was a dreamer.

Joseph remained a dreamer after being sold into bondage. And he held to the lofty honor of his dream, choosing to leave his garments behind to escape the lust of Potiphar's wife. That choice landed him in prison.

But Joseph was a dreamer in prison too. His interpretation of dreams got him out of that prison and put him in a position of power in Pharoah's palace. There the dreamer delivered two nations and was reunited with his family. He received a coat of honor from Pharoah and moved us one step closer to God's dream for our future. **Never forget:** You are a dreamer.

You Are (UR) --followers of God.

JANUARY 19 *(EPHESIANS 5:1,2)*

When my daughter was seven or eight months old *(just before she learned to walk)* I got a glimpse of God's heart that I will always treasure. She had a brand new walker and clear paths of access, exercise, investigation and speed through the house. One of those paths was to the front door and that was where I saw the Lord.

I came home in a hurry one day and found an obstruction behind the door. My bouncing baby was waiting for the object of her affection. The look in those big brown eyes was arresting -- debilitating -- empowering. My hurry evaporated and I stood there helpless and yet, capable of all things.

Agility was suddenly the order of the day, because she started to follow every step for a very long time. From that day forward, I hurried to hear those little feet traveling the path to that front door and remembered when I followed hard after God.

Gabrielle is older now. Adolescence is demanding its due. She, like me, must overcome the wicked one. (1 John 2:12-14) How I long for the day when we both know our Father and become followers of God as dear children.

You Are (UR) -- blessed!

JANUARY 20 *(DEUTERONOMY 28:3)*

You are blessed in the city and blessed in the field. (Deuteronomy 28: 3) Geography and situation have nothing to do with it. Think you're OK -- under the circumstances? Well, what are you doing under there? You are blessed. Still can't see it? Stop looking and listen to *(believe)* what God says. (Jeremiah 17:5-8) **Say it out loud:** I am blessed!

You Are (UR) -- extremely valuable.

(MATTHEW 10:28-31) JANUARY 21

I once worked for a retailer who said that a thing is worth what you can get for it. Once, he bought a half dozen inexpensive hammered dulcimers to sell as Christmas gifts. The price tag was just under $25 each. Those dulcimers sat in that store collecting dust for two years.

The third year he shined them up and marked them up to $125 each. They all sold in a week. Same dulcimers. Same store. Same customers. The only thing that changed was perceived value.

You are what you are, you have what you have, and you do what you do, based on what you believe is available and how much of it you believe you are worth. (Luke 15:11-31)

You might want to reread John 3:16 before you sell yourself cheap. God values you so highly that he has the hairs on your head numbered. And that's not just follicle count. Those are serial numbers. Forget DNA -- We're talking G • O • D.

President Abraham Lincoln once said, *"It is difficult to make a man miserable while he feels he is worthy of himself and claims kindred to the great God who made him."* You are extremely valuable.

"Courage [is] the determination not to be overwhelmed by any object, that power of the mind capable of sloughing off the thingification of the past."

Martin Luther King Jr.

You Are (UR) -- a curious kind of confident.

JANUARY 22 *(2 COR. 4:13-5:8)*

My phone rang at 1:30 AM. Willie Mae Kennedy, my next door neighbor and a member of my church, was dying. She had been battling cancer for a very long time and had outlived the doctors' prognosis by a long shot. We had every confidence that the God who had already healed her (Isaiah 53:3-5/1 Peter 2:24) would also raise her up. (James 5:14,15)

My wife and I laid hands on her and prayed fervently for almost an hour. She was fighting for every breath. There were many in the room who expected her to die, but even that was not discouraging. And then, the tide changed. Suddenly there was a calm that I am not equipped to describe. It was more than peace. It was a curious kind of confidence.

With my hand on her brow, Willie Mae left that body as calmly as a baby going to sleep. And, perhaps for the first time in my life, it was clear that we have somewhere else to go. No, I'm in no hurry to die. But oh to know that one day, I too will have this mortality swallowed up in immortality. That makes me a curious kind of confident.

You Are (UR) -- out of sight.

JANUARY 23 *(PSALM 27:4,5)*

You'd have to be a product of the 70's for that statement to hit you like I want it to without explanation. But suffice it to say: It's a good thing -- no matter how you read it. The devil can't kill you: **A.** Because he doesn't have the power. (Luke 10:19) **B.** Because he doesn't have the authority. (Colossians 2:13-15) **C.** Because he doesn't even know where your life is. (Colossians 3:1-3) **Bottom line:** No one can see the you that you see. They only see the you that your words authorize God to reveal to them. Agree with God about yourself and let everyone see the salvation of the Lord. (Psalm 50:23)

You Are (UR) -- powerful.

(LUKE 10:17-20) JANUARY 24

Aeschylus, the Greek tragic dramatist said, *"The man whose authority is recent is always stern."*

The disciples proved him true, five hundred years later. From desiring to call down fire like Elijah did, to marveling at fleeing devils and wanting to overthrow the Romans, they loved to see God move -- on anything and anyone that opposed them. It seems the tradition continues as many who have discovered that, through Jesus, they now possess the power of God, seek to destroy, overthrow, and acquire the possessions of their "enemies."

But Jesus warned them and us not to get carried away. *"You know not what Spirit you are of,"* he said to the would-be firebrands. (Luke 9:51-55) He reminded the seventy that the devil was defeated long ago, and that's not much to shout about. Being right with God is far better. (Luke 10:17-20)

And to the hopeful Roman overthrowers, he revealed true power. *"It is not for you to know the times and the seasons which the father has placed in his own hands."* (Acts 1:4-8 <esp. vs. 6>) *"Vengence is mine; I will repay, saith the Lord."* (Romans 12:19) *"But you shall receive power after that the Holy Ghost is come upon you. And you shall be witnesses...."* We came to seek and to save, not to condemn and destroy. (Luke 9:56) Now that's real power. And you are powerful.

"Courage is what it takes to stand up and speak; courage is what it takes to sit down and listen."

Winston Churchill

You Are (UR) -- the apple of God's eye.

JANUARY 25 *(DEUTERONOMY 32:10)*

"A word fitly spoken is like apples of gold in pictures of silver." You are a living manifestation of God's fitly spoken word. (Genesis 1:26) God values you. And He has promised to protect you.

Under the shadow of His wings God will hide you, from all who would harm you. (Psalm 17:8,9) And no one had better touch you. (Zechariah 7:6-8) *"For the eyes of the Lord run to and fro throughout the whole earth, to shew Himself strong in the behalf of them whose heart is perfect toward Him."* (2 Chronicles 16:9) And you are the *"apple of His eye."*

You Are (UR) -- free!

JANUARY 26 *(JOHN 8:31-36)*

When I fly, I love to see the seat belt light go off and hear the captain say, *"You are now free to move about the cabin."* I usually heed his or her warning to keep the seat belt fastened loosely around me and I very seldom get up and move. But I do like knowing that I can if I want to.

I like knowing that there are smooth skies ahead. I like knowing that everything is functioning properly. The comfort that comes from trusting the trained professionals at the helm, makes planes a great place to sit back and relax. Wherever I am in Jesus, I like knowing that I am free.

Some people, on the other hand, are terrified to even get on the plane -- forget about moving around while it's in the air. Their seat belts are tight and their knuckles are white. They are imprisoned, even in their freedom. Consider the irony, that, at least in the natural, we are all going to the same place. Some are going peacefully. Others are resisting a - rest.

You Are (UR) -- going to get your chance.

(MATTHEW 14:22-31) JANUARY 27

Funny thing about a chance to succeed -- it is also a chance to fail. And for those of us who have hoped and prayed and prepared and prodded as we waited patiently for opportunity to knock, there is always the slightest bit of hesitation to open the door when it (He) does. (Revelation 3:20)

Why? The *'am I worthy'* monster. The *'can I do it'* committee. Give it any name you like. Failure's greatest success is in getting us not to try -- hopefully not at all, but definitely not again.

Moses struggled with his own inability and argued with God when called to lead the children of Israel out of Egypt. (Exodus 3/4:1-17) His protests seem downright insane when reading them thousands of years later. And yet, we sit reading when we too should be doing. Why? Same spirit, a few thousand years older and wiser.

Can you do it? No you can't. But 1 Thessalonians 5:24 & Philippians 2:13 are crystal clear. *"Faithful is he that calleth you, who also will do it."* *"For it is God which worketh in you both to will and to do of his good pleasure."* You are going to get your chance.

You Are (UR) -- called to be a saint.

(1 CORINTHIANS 1:1-3) JANUARY 28

"To be or not to be?"

There is never any question for those who are called to be. For the gifts and callings of God are without repentance. He said it. He meant it. And we're here to represent it. We are called to be saints. And by the grace of God, we are walking worthy of the vocation wherewith we are called.

You Are (UR) -- a living soul.

JANUARY 29 *(GENESIS 2:7)*

Adam and Eve established a pattern in the garden of Eden that continues to affect us all. I'm not talking about the sin nature. I'm talking about the human condition of being created to be one thing and becoming something else.

When God said; *"let us make man,"* he was not at all vague about what man would be. *"Let us make man in our image, after our likeness."* He was just as clear about man's position of authority in the earth, his job description and his relationships. *"Let them have dominion over the fish of the sea, and over the fowl of the air, and over the cattle, and over all the earth, and over every creeping thing that creepeth upon the earth."*

God, the author and the finisher of our faith, doesn't just dream up projects and leave them unfinished. He is Alpha and Omega, the beginning and the ending. It is he that works in us both to will and to do of his good pleasure. (Philippians 2:12,13) And we can be confident of this very thing, that he which has begun a good work in us, will perform it until the day of Jesus Christ. (Philippians 1:6)

So, God created man. And he created him just as he planned. *"In his own image."* It is therefore extremely important to understand that our sinful nature and consequent behavior is not due to manufacturer's error. God made us right. God made us perfect. God made us just like he planned. So what happened?

The creation of man appears to have been a process rather than an instantaneous work. God formed Adam of the dust of the ground, but there he sat, inanimate and lifeless. Then God breathed into his nostrils the breath of life; *"and man became a living soul."* (Genesis 2:7)

Life is a wonderful state of being. Solomon said that in the land of the living *"there is hope"* and *"a living dog is better than a dead lion."* (Ecclesiastes 9:4) But just living is not enough for God. Simple animation was a far cry from what he envisioned. The creation process was not complete. Godly love desired that man be allowed to find his way, as it were, to the Tree of Life and eat that which would bring perfect, abundant, eternal life. But something happened -- along the way.

You Are (UR) -- a living soul. *(continued)*

(GENESIS 2:7) JANUARY 30

How often we face the trials that happen -- along the way. From the children of Israel in the wilderness to distraught disciples on a raging sea, (Exodus13:17 / Mark 4:35-41) time and again God declares a thing concerning us and sends us on our way. But along the way, other voices arise, denying the declaration of God. We are forced to choose. Do I believe God? Or do I believe my circumstances? Am I what God says I am? Or will I choose to become something else? The first Adam made a choice that required the work of the last Adam.

The subtile serpent entered the garden and began a conversation with Eve. There are three statements here that will haunt mankind from here on. First a question. *"Hast God said?"* Adam's dilemna is our dilemna. Did God make a declaration about your life and do you know what it is?

Romans 10:13-17 teaches that *"whosoever shall call on the name of the Lord shall be saved."* That's pretty straight forward until you read further. *"How then shall they call on him in whom they have not believed? and how shall they believe in him of whom they have not heard? and how shall they hear without a preacher? And how shall they preach except they be sent?"* Sent. Authorized. Commissioned with a word from God.

The foundation of all preaching is what God said. Paul said, *"I am not ashamed of the gospel of Christ: for it is the power of God unto salvation to every one that believeth; to the Jew first, and to the Greek. For therein is the righteousness of God revealed from faith to faith: as it is written, The just shall live by faith."* (Romans 1:16,17) Righteousness -- what is right for my life, is defined by what God said.

Salvation and freedom from condemnation of sin are right. Because God said so. Healing and health and victory over sickness and disease are right. Because God said so. Prosperity and deliverance from poverty are right. Because God said so.

You Are (UR) -- a living soul. *(continued)*

JANUARY 31 *(GENESIS 2:7)*

Eve responded to the serpent's inquiry. *"We may eat of the fruit of the trees of the garden: But of the fruit of the tree which is in the midst of the garden, God hath said, Ye shall not eat of it, neither shall ye touch it, lest ye die."* Another precedent was set. There were two trees in the midst of the garden. God said don't touch one, but they had free access to the other. The word *"don't"* gripped their focus. Like the prohibitive red beam at an intersection, a traffic signal became a stop light. They could no longer see the Tree of Life.

"You shall not surely die." The serpent found his opening. God said one thing, but what did he really mean? Eve hesitated and Adam was silent and we were sold into sin. *"For God doth know...."* Suddenly, he who created us out of a loving heart is an adversary. He who declares, *"For I know the thoughts that I think toward you, saith the Lord, thoughts of peace, and not of evil, to give you an expected end."* is a foe. (Jeremiah 29:11) God, our Father, has become a suspect enemy.

They ate of the tree. Their eyes were opened. They knew they were naked. They were ashamed. And when they heard the voice of the Lord walking in the garden, they hid themselves. But God would ask two questions that point the way back to him. *"Where art thou?"* Where indeed? Are we hiding from God because we are feeling naked and afraid? And if we feel that way, God wonders, *"Who told you that you were naked?"* Who have you been listening to that has caused you to doubt and fear me? Adam and Eve established a pattern in the garden of Eden that continues to affect us all.

Adam set one more important precedent. Adam & Eve were the first recipients of God's grace. They were the reason for God's first sacrifice. Covered by the bloody skins of slain animals and spared the wrath of a holy God, they were evicted from the Garden of Eden -- as a safeguard. God sealed the way to the Tree of Life with Cherubims and a flaming sword so they could not eat of it and seal their sin in eternity. Why? Because God blessed them. (Genesis 1:28) And what God has blessed, no man can curse. (Numbers 22:12) You are Adam's offspring.

You Are (UR) -- not your own.

{Taken directly from Oswald Chambers' -- My Utmost for His Highest 11/1}

(1 CORINTHIANS 6:19) FEBRUARY 1

"Know ye not that . . . ye are not your own?" 1 COR. 6:19

There is no such thing as a private life— *"a world within the world"* — for a man or woman who is brought into fellowship with Jesus Christ's sufferings. God breaks up the private life of His saints, and makes it a thoroughfare for the world on the one hand and for Himself on the other. No human being can stand that unless he is identified with Jesus Christ.

We are not sanctified for ourselves, we are called into the fellowship of the Gospel, and things happen which have nothing to do with us, God is getting us into fellowship with Himself. Let Him have His way, if you do not, instead of being of the slightest use to God in His redemptive work in the world, you will be a hindrance and a clog.

{Our sincerest thanks to Oswald Chambers for inspiring us daily.}

You Are (UR) -- the whether man.

(1 KINGS 18:41-45) FEBRUARY 2

Today is Groundhog Day. And tradition admonishes us to rely on the shadow of Punxutawney Phil and his rodent relations to determine how much longer winter will last.

Thank God we abide under the shadow of the Almighty and whether winter lasts six more weeks or six more years, it will have no bearing on the seasons of our lives.

The weather man can report what he sees. You, on the other hand, can declare what God says. And that makes you -- the whether man.

You Are (UR) -- redeemed.

FEBRUARY 3 *(GALATIANS 3:13,14)*

We were all born sinners. It's sad but true. What's even sadder is that many, in their attempt to explain it, will characterize that condition as manufacturer's error. God, being omnipotent, omniscient, omnipresent, and all, He must have made us that way.

But James 1:17 tells us that every good gift and every perfect gift is from above and comes from the Father of lights, with whom is no variableness, neither shadow of turning. God made you good.

What happened to us, was that Adam sold us into sin (Romans 7:14) and it was the new owner *(the devil)* that messed us up, through misuse. (i.e., *...the body is not for fornication, but for the Lord.* 1 Corinthians 6:13) The good news is, you have been redeemed -- bought back -- repossessed -- purchased by the blood of the Lamb.

You are like a skateboard bought with grandma's Green Stamps. *(I always found it odd that they called it The S&H Green Stamps Redemption Center.)* Now the Lord wants to unwrap you from your bondage, dust you off, repair what's broken or missing, and get you back to your intended purpose. (Jeremiah 29:10-14 esp. vs. 11)

You Are (UR) -- taking a turn for the better.

FEBRUARY 4 *(ACTS 3:25,26)*

Do you feel turned around - disoriented - out of sorts - not like yourself? It makes you uncomfortable - doesn't it? Well, there is a cause and constant in the turmoil. You keep adjusting so that Jesus remains in front of you. And he keeps moving so that your sins remain behind you. Thank God you're feeling less like yourself. It's probably because you are becoming more like Him.

You Are (UR) -- more excellent than your neighbor.

(*PROVERBS 12:26*) FEBRUARY 5

My wife grew up on a farm in rural North Carolina. Her grandmother sent her to school every day with homemade country ham biscuits for lunch. *(Grandma is 98 and still makes biscuits every morning.)*

But the kids at school teased Gloria so badly, about being a country girl, that she started trashing her biscuits on the way to school and drinking milk or juice for lunch while she watched with envy as the 'cool' kids dined on baloney on 'Wonder' bread. Sound like the silly antics of a kid? What heaven-made treasures are you trashing each day because you have been seduced by the ways of the wicked?

You Are (UR) -- just seventeen (17") inches from "there".

(*ROMANS 10:8-10*) FEBRUARY 6

I'm told that seventeen inches is about the distance from your heart to your mouth.

> *"With the heart man believes unto righteousness and with the mouth confession is made unto salvation."*

That's salvation from condemnation for sin. Salvation from sickness and disease. Salvation from poverty and lack. And salvation from all of life's calamities.

Believe it or not, what you believe in your heart (Romans 10:13-17) is controlling what you say with your mouth. (Matthew 12:34) And say what you want, you are always going to wind up wherever you keep on saying you're going to wind up. (Mark 11:22-24) **Say it out loud!** I'm just seventeen inches from "there!"

You Are (UR) -- light in the Lord.

FEBRUARY 7 *(EPHESIANS 5:8-13)*

I've heard it said that you do what you are. Well, you are light -- in the Lord. You used to be darkness, but now are you light, and the instructions from the manufacturer are clear. *"Walk as children of light."*

You are proving and reproving what is and is not acceptable unto the Lord. Jesus compared you to a city that is set on a hill that cannot be hid. *"Let your light so shine before men,"* he said, *"that they may see your good works and glorify your father which is in heaven."* (Matthew 5:16)

Men may see your good works, but light will also expose evil works. Proving and reproving, you cannot have it both ways. *"The light of the body is the eye: if therefore thine eye be single, thy whole body shall be full of light, but if thine eye be evil, thy whole body shall be full of darkness. If therefore the light that is in thee be darkness, how great is that darkness!"* (Matthew 6:22,23)

But you are light in the Lord. You used to be darkness, but now are you light. *"This then is the message which we have heard of him, and declare unto you, that God is light, and in him is no darkness at all. If we say that we have fellowship with him and walk in darkness, we lie, and do not the truth: But if we walk in the light, as he is in the light, we have fellowship one with another and the blood of Jesus Christ his Son cleanseth us from all sin."* (1 John 1:5-7) You are light in the Lord.

---

*"Never let your head hang down.
Never give up and sit and grieve.
Find another way. And don't pray when it rains if
you don't pray when the sun shines."*

Satchel Paige

You Are (UR) -- fulfilling the law of God.

They are called The Ten Commandments and we have set them up, engraved in stone, as prohibitions on human behavior. But that is the carnal man's way. Read them again with a renewed heart and you will see that God never said don't. Instead he said what we shall do, expecting the finished work of Christ in us.

When David proclaims, *"I shall not die, but live, and declare the works of the Lord."* (Psalm 118:17), there is no doubt that he is rejoicing in God's promise of longevity. Hezekiah heard no commandment to go to the temple when Isaiah declared God's change of heart. (2 Kings 20:1-5) What he heard was a promise of his spared life. He didn't have to go. He could go.

"Thou shalt have no other gods before me."

Hallelujah! I do not. Jesus made it so. He is the way, the truth, and the life. It is by him and him alone that I have found my way to the one and true living God. Where else would I go? He has the words of eternal life.

I used to worship whatever accommodated the lustful desires of my lost life. No law engraved in stone could alter my desires or my behavior. Then Jesus came. He made me a new creature and in me, fulfilled the law of God. (2 Corinthians 5:17) God was right. He called me what I would be before I was. I have no other gods before him. His love is in me. Now I love him. I am fulfilling the law of God.

"Hope awakens courage. He who can implant courage in the human soul is the best physician."

Karl Ludwig von Knebel

You Are (UR) -- fulfilling the law of God.

FEBRUARY 9 *(ROMANS 13:10)*

They are called The Ten Commandments and we have set them up, engraved in stone, as prohibitions on human behavior. But that is the carnal man's way. Read them again with a renewed heart and you will see that God never said don't. Instead he declared what we shall do, expecting the finished work of Christ in us. (Exodus 20)

> *"Thou shalt not make unto thee any graven image, or any likeness of anything that is in heaven above; or that is in the earth beneath, or that is in the water under the earth. Thou shalt not bow down thyself to them, nor serve them: for I the Lord thy God am a jealous God, visiting the iniquity of the fathers upon the children unto the third and fourth generation of them that hate me; And shewing mercy unto thousands of them that love me, and keep my commandments."*

Like the Epicureans and Stoics on Mars' hill, modern day disciples of Darwin encourage us to align ourselves with creation rather than worship the creator, giving him thanks. (Acts 17:22-30 / Romans 1:18-32) Evolution they say. Revolution we pray. Change is the order of the day.

Yes we once bowed down to lesser gods, denying our Father in heaven. But though we deny Him, He cannot deny Himself. (2 Timothy 2:12,13) His amazing love has drawn us back and now we must cry: *"Who is like unto thee, oh Lord among the Gods? Who is like unto thee, glorious in holiness, fearful in praises, doing wonders?"* (Exodus 15:11)

"For though there be that are called gods, whether in heaven or in earth, (as there be gods many, and lords many,) But to us there is but one God, the Father, of whom are all things, and we in him; and one Lord Jesus Christ, by whom are all things, and we by him." (1 Corinthians 8:5,6)

Indeed, the law has found its place in our hearts. We shall not make any graven images, nor bow ourselves down to lesser gods. We are fulfilling the law of God.

You Are (UR) -- fulfilling the law of God.

(ROMANS 13:10) FEBRUARY 10

They are called The Ten Commandments and we have set them up, engraved in stone, as prohibitions on human behavior. But that is the carnal man's way. Read them again with a renewed heart and you will see that God never said don't. Instead he declared what we shall do, expecting the finished work of Christ in us. (Exodus 20)

"Thou shalt not take the name of the Lord thy God in vain."

Say it out loud! No! I shall not. *"The name of the Lord is a strong tower."* (Proverbs 18:10) He has made me righteous. I have run into it and am safe. *"He that troubleth his own house shall inherit the wind."* Why would I ever take such a refuge in vain? It seems so simple, now that his law is written in my heart. (Hebrews 10:16,17) I am fulfilling the law of God.

You Are (UR) -- sitting pretty.

(EPHESIANS 2:1-6) FEBRUARY 11

At the game, at the theater, in a restaurant or at church; you've got the best seat in the house. Most pay extra for it. Some arrive early and even camp out overnight to beat the lines. And yes, there are those who beg, borrow, barter, lie, cheat, steal, scheme, smile and schmooze, just to obtain that special spot.

But Jesus died and rose again to give you what human effort alone simply cannot attain. From where you sit in Him, you can see and hear everything. (Hebrews 4:11-13) All that you need is near you (Romans 10:8-10) and there is an uncanny sense of power. (Luke 10:19) You just can't beat the perspective from a heavenly vantage point. And you've got it.

You Are (UR) -- fulfilling the law of God.

FEBRUARY 12 *(ROMANS 13:10)*

They are called The Ten Commandments and we have set them up, engraved in stone, as prohibitions on human behavior. But that is the carnal man's way. Read them again with a renewed heart and you will see that God never said don't. Instead he declared what we shall do, expecting the finished work of Christ in us. (Exodus 20)

> *"Remember the sabbath day and keep it holy."*

Christ finished his work. (John 17:4) But we are still working. Working out our salvation with fear and trembling. (Philippians 2:12,13) Day by day, we are walking in the good works that God has before ordained for us. We are laboring in a cursed earth that puts up a mighty good fight. The sweat of our brow and the pain of labor are constant reminders that what God promised -- what Jesus finished -- was very necessary work. (Genesis 3:14,15)

And then, there is a rest. There is the rest that remains for the people of God. And we labor to enter in. Our regular sabbaths from daily endeavors are God's confirmation that *"he that entered into his rest, he also hath ceased from his own works, as God did from his."* (Hebrews 4:1-11)

How precious is that sabbath? It is God's gift, made for man, not man for it. (Mark 2:27,28) It is a gift that says, *"Come unto me, all ye that labor and are heavy laden, and I will give you rest. Take my yoke upon you, and learn of me, for I am meek and lowly in heart: and ye shall find rest unto your souls. For my yoke is easy, and my burden is light."* (Matthew 11:28-30) And we are keeping it as it is kept in us. We are fulfilling the law of God.

"Courage is one step ahead of fear."

Coleman Young

You Are (UR) -- fulfilling the law of God.

(ROMANS 13:10) FEBRUARY 13

They are called The Ten Commandments and we have set them up, engraved in stone, as prohibitions on human behavior. But that is the carnal man's way. Read them again with a renewed heart and you will see that God never said don't. Instead he declared what we shall do, expecting the finished work of Christ in us. (Exodus 20)

> *"Honor thy father and thy mother; that thy days may be long upon the land which the Lord thy God giveth thee."*

This is the first commandment with promise. (Ephesians 6:1-2) A contingency. If you do this, then that will happen. That's a pretty good deal. Obey, respect, and spend time with mom and dad and I get to live longer and better. I wish I had known earlier.

Now I tell my daughter: the principle ingredient is for you to be obedient. And now that God is my heavenly father, this is not difficult at all. This is the love of God, that we keep his commandments: and his commandments are not grievous. (1 John 5:3) We are fulfilling the law of God.

You Are (UR) -- loved.

(JOHN 3:16) FEBRUARY 14

Absolutely, positively, without question, undoubtedly, irrevocably, unequivocally, indisputably, more than you'll ever be -- loved. (1 John 3:16) Jesus crossed his heart and died with hope that you would someday be his. Happy Valentine's Day.

You Are (UR) -- sitting on a gold mine.

FEBRUARY 15 *(PHILIPPIANS 2:12,13)*

It is yours to excavate. It is yours to work out. Or you might say; *"It's mine."* If you are standing by the gate gazing at greener pastures, dreaming of things you might acquire that will fill the void that is 'causing your dissatisfaction or failure;' work is going undone. You are neglecting the gift. (1 Timothy 4:11-16/Romans 8:32) **Note:** God never told us to work out our problems. He told us to work out our salvation.

You Are (UR) -- fulfilling the law of God.

FEBRUARY 16 *(ROMANS 13:10)*

They are called The Ten Commandments and we have set them up, engraved in stone, as prohibitions on human behavior. But that is the carnal man's way. Read them again with a renewed heart and you will see that God never said don't. Instead he declared what we shall do, expecting the finished work of Christ in us. (Exodus 20)

"Thou shalt not kill."

The world has grown very sophisticated. No more shoot outs at the OK Corral. Murder and hatred still occur but the majority of it never makes the six-o-clock news. It's more internal and orchestrated. (Matthew 5:21,22) Like the Jews and the Samaritans, people just have *"no dealings"* with the objects of their ire. (John 4:1-9)

But the law of love is at work in your heart. The fire of God is melting what would otherwise grow cold as stone. (Matthew 24:12 / Romans 12:18-21) Tumults and terrorists are an increasing inevitability, but they are no match for the grace, mercy, longsuffering and love that you have witnessed. You are fulfilling the law of God.

You Are (UR) -- fulfilling the law of God.

(ROMANS 13:10) FEBRUARY 17

They are called The Ten Commandments and we have set them up, engraved in stone, as prohibitions on human behavior. But that is the carnal man's way. Read them again with a renewed heart and you will see that God never said don't. Instead he declared what we shall do, expecting the finished work of Christ in us. (Exodus 20)

"Thou shalt not commit adultery."

In a bed or in your head (heart), adultery is the direct result of not understanding. Adulterers don't understand the intimate bond between a man and his wife. And more importantly, they don't understand that they can't understand it. (Proverbs 30:18-20) Adulterous attraction comes from a desire to experience what others appear to have. But that is a thing that cannot be experienced. You can't have the puppy in the window.

Adulterers certainly don't understand the rage their intrusion generates in God and man. Crimes of passion are nothing to play with. (Proverbs 6:32-35) God is a jealous God. Adulterers don't understand the original intent of God. (Matthew 19:1-9)

Adultery occurs when people don't understand the importance of submission to authority and the supernatural power of unified willing obedience. (1 Corinthians 7:1-5) But you understand because you stand under the word, love and authority of the most high God. You are faithful to Him and He is faithful to you. You are fulfilling the law of God.

"Courage and perseverance have a magical talisman, before which difficulties disappear and obstacles vanish into air."

John Quincy Adams

You Are (UR) -- fulfilling the law of God.

FEBRUARY 18 *(ROMANS 13:10)*

They are called The Ten Commandments and we have set them up, engraved in stone, as prohibitions on human behavior. But that is the carnal man's way. Read them again with a renewed heart and you will see that God never said don't. Instead he declared what we shall do, expecting the finished work of Christ in us. (Exodus 20)

"Thou shalt not steal."

Agur, son of Jakeh prayed, *"...give me neither poverty nor riches; feed me with food convenient for me: Lest I be full, and deny thee, and say Who is the Lord? or lest I be poor, and steal, and take the name of my God in vain."* (Proverbs 30:7-9) Well Praise God: Rich, poor, or as DeTocqueville so accurately predicted, "the neither rich nor poor majority:" we who stole, need steal no more (Ephesians 4:28) -- especially not from the Lord. (Malachi 3:8-12) For he meets all our need according to his riches in glory by Christ Jesus. (Philippians 4:19)

Now, regardless of our earthly holdings, we can trust in the living God, who giveth us richly all things to enjoy. We can do good, and be rich in good works, ready to distribute, willing to communicate (give), Laying up in store for ourselves a good foundation against the time to come, that we may lay hold on eternal life. (1 Timothy 6:17-19) Steal? I don't think so. You are fulfilling the law of God.

"One isn't necessarily born with courage, but one is born with potential. Without courage, we cannot practice any other virtue with consistency. We can't be kind, true, merciful, generous, or honest."

Maya Angelou

You Are (UR) -- fulfilling the law of God.

(ROMANS 13:10) FEBRUARY 19

They are called The Ten Commandments and we have set them up, engraved in stone, as prohibitions on human behavior. But that is the carnal man's way. Read them again with a renewed heart and you will see that God never said don't. Instead he declared what we shall do, expecting the finished work of Christ in us. (Exodus 20)

"Thou shalt not bear false witness against thy neighbor."

You are a witness. (Acts 1:8) You have no lies to tell. (1 John 1:1-4) Your news is good news and your expectation of people is God's expectation. (Jeremiah 29:11) No mother-of-Jabez misnomers for you. (1 Chronicles 4:9) You call those things which be not as though they were. (Romans 4:16,17) You are a true witness. And a true witness delivers souls. (Proverbs 14:25) You are fulfilling the law of God.

You Are (UR) -- a keeper.

(MATTHEW 13:47,48) FEBRUARY 20

Any fisherman's first decision, upon catching a fish is: Is it fit to keep? Keep, meaning not only the opposite of not discarding, but also to protect and preserve until he can get it home. Don't look now, but you have been caught. (Phillipians 3:9-12) And God intends to keep you. Bass and Bream keep well -- well -- in a live well. Fish like you and me have to be kept in our souls *(our mind, emotions, and will - our psuché / Greek for soul denoting the breath of life)*. As Adam was instructed to keep *(garrison about with armed guards on fortified walls)* the garden, so likewise, God who has caught and decided to keep us -- keeps us. He keeps our hearts and minds. (Philippians 4:6-8) He keeps us in perfect peace. (Isaiah 26:3) He keeps us from evil. (2 Chronicles 4:9,10/Matthew 6:9-13) He keeps His promises. (Numbers 23:19)

You Are (UR) -- nobody's fool.

FEBRUARY 21 *(EPH. 5:14-17)*

At least, that's how we say it now: now that we've been educated. On the playground, however, it was: *"My mama didn't raise no fool."* Either way, fools just don't seem to see what's going on around them. Consequently, they waste precious time because they simply don't have a clue what God wants for their lives. But not you -- oh wise and powerful one. You know that God doesn't want anyone to perish, so you make the most of your time trying to win souls. (Proverbs 11:30,31) Say amen.

You Are (UR) -- fulfilling the law of God.

FEBRUARY 22 *(ROMANS 13:10)*

They are called The Ten Commandments and we have set them up, engraved in stone, as prohibitions on human behavior. But that is the carnal man's way. Read them again with a renewed heart and you will see that God never said don't. Instead he declared what we shall do, expecting the finished work of Christ in us. (Exodus 20)

> *"Thou shalt not covet thy neighbor's house,*
> *thou shalt not covet thy neighbor's wife, nor his manservant,*
> *nor his maidservant, nor his ox, nor his ass,*
> *nor any thing that is thy neighbor's."*

The Lord is your shepherd. You shall not want. (Psalm 23) You are content with such things as you have. (1 Timothy 6:6-8) And you know that your God shall supply all your need according to his riches in glory by Christ Jesus. (Philippians 4:19) Paul declared; "I have coveted no man's silver, or gold, or apparel" He went on to say that his hands had ministered unto his necessities, and to them that were with him. He knew, like you, that "it is more blessed to give than to receive." (Acts 20:33-35) You love your neighbor as yourself. (Luke 10:25-27) You are fulfilling the law of God.

You Are (UR) -- bone of his bone and flesh of his flesh.

(EPHESIANS 5:21-33) FEBRUARY 23

The "mystery" of marriage reveals the miracle of Christ and the church. But in a country where the divorce rate seems out of control, perhaps we need a revelation of that mysterious miracle. We are *"members of his body, of his flesh, and of his bones."* With that in mind, some things are needful -- even required -- for the mystery to unfold and the miracle to manifest. Could unfeigned love and reverent submission be born of qualities we have been taught to avoid? Selfishness. Jealousy. Narrow mindedness. The negative connotations leave when our eyes are opened to the fact that we are one. When God looked on his creation -- man: *"Male and female created he them; and blessed them, and called their name Adam, in the day when they were created."* (Genesis 5:1,2) In the mystery of marriage, God saw the miracle of Christ and the church. We are one. We are bone of his bone and flesh of his flesh.

You Are (UR) --selfish.

(MARK 10:17-22) FEBRUARY 24

The rich young ruler has taken the proverbial *"bum rap"* for much too long. All this time we have faulted him for being greedy -- selfish. But the cause of his closed hand runs deeper than we once suspected. When compared to Luke's report of the same encounter a not so common view is revealed. The lawyer of chapter 10:25-27 highlights the question of boundaries. A qualified definition of: self. *"And who is my neighbor?"* he asks. His selfishness would have been grand, celebrated, heralded throughout the ages as generosity, had he accurately defined self. Isn't it odd that the people that we fault most for *"selfishness"* are wonderful providers for the members of their *"inner circle"* It's just that we are, all too often, not in said circle. It is actually the grandeur of their largess that generally causes us to hurl the accusation to begin with. And so, on a scale large or small: there is plenty going around. The problems arise over who should have it. Consider the concept a sort of living *"For Whom The Bell Tolls."* Negative connotations notwithstanding, just as the sun is measured by candle power, love for others is measured by love for self -- self/ish/ness. And you are selfish.

You Are (UR) --jealous.

FEBRUARY 25 *(1 COR. 3:18-21)*

The power of the possessive is the power of God. You are His and He is yours. (Song of Solomon 6:3 / 7:10) Children get it early on. And ours must be childlike faith. *"Mine!"* They say it without a second thought. It is us who have lost our hold on God's gift. *"All things are yours."* This takes the *"advantage"* (Jude 16) of men's person out of the picture. *"Whether Paul, or Apollos, or Cephas, or the world, or life, or death, or things present, or things to come, all are yours; And ye are Christ's, and Christ is God's."*

God makes no apologies for his possessive passion. *"I the Lord thy God am a jealous God,"* he says, in Exodus 20:5. Exodus 34:14 calls his name, Jealous, and reemphasizes his jealousy. Jesus, *"thought it not robbery to be equal with God"* and we are instructed to *"let this mind"* be in us, also. (Philippians 2:5-11)

Jealousy signifies surrender - naked and unashamed love. I love my wife. I want to be with her. If I can't be with her, I want to know where she is, who she's with, what she's doing, and when she's coming back. I'm the same way with my daughter, my God, and every one or thing I love. From the tabernacle, to the cross, to the communion table, there is great power in jealous weakness born of love. (Numbers 5:11-31 / Acts 1:1-3 / 1 Corinthians 11:23-32) It is power that you possess. **Say it out loud!** I am jealous!

You Are (UR) -- a witness.

FEBRUARY 26 *(ACTS 1:8)*

True or False? (Proverbs 14:25) **T/F** - You have seen something. (Psalm 34:8) **T/F** - You have heard something. (Romans 10:17) **T/F** - You know something. (1 John 5:13) Are you willing to testify? (Revelation 12:10-12)

You Are (UR) --narrow minded.

(MATTHEW 7:13,14) FEBRUARY 27

"Singleness of vision and thorough oneness with his age is a mark of the successful man. It is as though Nature must needs make men narrow in order to give them force."
W.E.B. DuBois -- *The Souls of Black Folk*

"Power comes from results which is the product of narrowly focusing on one thing."
Tom Peters -- The Pursuit of WOW!

"Brethren, I count not myself to have apprehended: but this one thing I do, forgetting those things which are behind, and reaching forth unto those things which are before, I press toward the mark for the prize of the high calling of God in Christ Jesus."
Paul the Apostle -- The Epistle to the Philippians 3:13,14

These guys are good, but our Lord is best.

"Enter ye in at the strait gate: for wide is the gate, and broad is the way, that leadeth to destruction and many there be which go in thereat. Because strait is the gate, and narrow is the way, which leadeth unto life, and few there be that find it."
Jesus -- The Gospel According to Matthew 7:13,14

People, things, and the devil himself, may try to distract you. But you are narrow minded.

You Are (UR) -- surrounded.

(PSALM 139:1-14) FEBRUARY 28

You may as well surrender. (John 6:66-68) Drop your weapons. (James 1:18-21) And get your hands up where I can see them. (1 Timothy 2:8) Now dance!! (Psalm 150:4)

You Are (UR) -- taking a leap of faith.

FEBRUARY 29 *(LUKE 1:39-41)*

When a growing John the Baptist heard the voice of Mary who was carrying Jesus, the Spirit of God moved him. He leaped in Elizabeth's womb and she was filled with the Holy Ghost. Truly, Christ was in Mary, John's hope of glory. (Colossians 1:27)

We too have heard the word from faithful stewards of the mysteries of God. (1 Corinthians 4:1,2) And like King David of old, and the disciples on the road to Emmaus, (Psalm 39:3 / Luke 24:13-32) our hearts burn and there is nothing left to do but leap for joy. (2 Samuel 6:16)

You Are (UR) -- married / subject to Christ.

MARCH 1 *(EPHESIANS 5:22,23)*

You are (UR) -- selfish, jealous and narrow minded, are what most would consider, negative headings. But I started the *"series"* with the idea that You Are (UR) -- bone of his bone and flesh of his flesh. I hope you can see that these ideas and many others get their life from our concept of who we are and consequently, who we believe our *"neighbor"* is.

The larger our circle of love, the less negative these ideas become. The purer our concept of unity / union, the more powerful selfishness, jealousy and narrow mindedness become. They increase in desirability more and more as we become comfortable members of the *"one new man"* described in Ephesians 2.

We are married. We are subject to Christ. Our love for him demands and creates love for others. And it demands that we love them *"as"* ourselves. Truly, the mystery of marriage reveals the miracle of Christ and the church.

You Are (UR) -- forgetting something.

(PHILIPPIANS 3:13,14) MARCH 2

I do realize that those words are a jolt to the memory, but don't bother trying to remember. Much of what you are forgetting needs to be forgotten. I'm talking about your past: past hurts, disappointments, failures and fears. Forgetting is an involuntary act usually associated with aging senility, but it is really just a by-product of not remembering. Or as a patriarch from the movie *"Avalon"* put it when questioned by a bored grandchild about why he told the same story every Thanksgiving: *"If you don't remember -- you forget."* This theory is especially effective if you define remember as the direct opposite of dismembering. In other words, the only way to forget what has happened to you is to stop reassembling it every time the devil brings you a piece of it. **Remember:** You've got a mark to hit. You can't see it if you're looking back.

You Are (UR) -- going where God wants you to.

(JONAH 1-4) MARCH 3

You can go peacefully, or you can go resisting arrest. You can go willingly and obediently and eat the fat of the land (Isaiah 1:19), or you can wither and die along the way, not seeing the good around you. (Jeremiah 17:5-8) You can rejoice in the deliverance that your faithfulness brings to others, (1 Timothy 4:11-16) or you can be buried with them as they die in their sins. But you're going where God wants you to. (Psalm 37:23)

PS Jonah could have booked first class passage to Nineveh as soon as he heard from the Lord. Instead, he went "Whale Class" and arrived smelling of krill and seaweed.

You Are (UR) -- covered.

MARCH 4 *(ROMANS 4:7)*

I trust you started the day with the blood of the lamb. It is the world's best cleanser. (Hebrews 9:22) Of course you applied some oil -- the anointing of the Holy Ghost. This gives you beauty for ashes and glory for your shame. (Isaiah 61:1-3) He's also quite the comforter. If you're feeling a little heavy -- put on the garment of praise.

It's no secret that a robe of righteousness is a victor's undergarment. (Luke 15:22) Breastplate of righteousness, girdle of truth, feet shod with the gospel of peace, helmet of salvation, shield of faith, and sword of the Spirit. (Ephesians 6:10-13) Angels to the right. Angels to the left. (Hebrews 1:13,14) A great cloud of witnesses hovering above you. (Hebrews 12:1) The Lord himself before you and the God of Israel is your rear guard. (Isaiah 52:12) The only place left for the devil is under your feet. (Luke 10:19) Step lively.

You Are (UR) -- the righteousness of God in Christ Jesus.

MARCH 5 *(2 CORINTHIANS 5:21)*

Let's face it, sinners don't read the Bible. Sinners read the church. People in the world don't seem to know right from wrong, up from down, or good from bad. (Isaiah 5:20) They think sickness and disease, poverty and lack, lewdness and immorality, etc..., etc..., ad infinitum, are normal and inevitable.

It's such stinkin' thinkin' that provokes statements like *"The kids are going to have sex before marriage no matter what we do, so we may as well teach them how to have 'safe' sex."* That's the way you talk when you have no hope and are without God in the world. (Ephesians 2:11-13) But when they see the abundant life of Christ in you -- not your own righteousness (Titus 3:3-5) -- they'll have proof positive of the good, acceptable, and perfect will of God. (Romans 12:1,2)

You Are (UR) -- a human being -- not a human doing.

Loretta LaRoughe

(GENESIS 2:7) MARCH 6

When God blew the breath of life into Adam's nostrils, he became a living soul. When you acknowledged you were a sinner *(not that you were doing sinful things)*, asked God to forgive you, and accepted Jesus as Lord of your life -- so did you. You became something. You didn't accomplish anything. Someone accomplished you. (Ephesians 2:8-10)

God told Moses that His name is -- I AM. But just as people insist on calling me Mike, when I just told them my name is Michael, we insist on calling God -- You Do. Yes, God does things. Psalm 150 encourages us to *"Praise him for his mighty acts."* And there are certainly things for us to do. Saul's second question on the road to Damascus was *"what wilt thou have me to do?"* But I'm glad he was mature enough to ask who was talking to him first. And it is just like Jesus to begin the answer with a name change. From that day forward, everything Paul the Apostle *did* -- came out of who he had *become*. (Acts 26:1-23 esp. vs 19)

You Are (UR) -- working with the best.

(2 CORINTHIANS 6:1) MARCH 7

It helps to have good co-workers. Not only do they cover you when you are not at your best, but they tend to bring the best out of you. (Philippians 2:12,13) In the best of situations, diversity tends to be the order of the day. *(Sports, The Arts, Universities, The Space Program, etc...)* There is not only the commonality of our shared talent, but the participants often come from any and everywhere. (Revelation 7:9)

Unfortunately, increased diversity usually means increased tension, (Acts 15:1-20) but it also means increased productivity. (1 Corinthians 15:9,10) And insecurity can enter in as well. You may wonder: *"How did I get here?"* or *"Do I deserve to be here?"* **Always remember:** You got here by grace and you deserve to be in hell. But then again, so does everyone else. And you are working with the best.

You Are (UR) -- going through hell.

MARCH 8 *(JOHN 11:1-4)*

GOOD! At least you are not going to hell. Don't stop for gas. *"Many are the afflictions of the righteous: but the Lord delivers him out of them all."* (Psalm 34:19) The key words here are *out of* -- the Lord tends to deliver *out of*, rather than *from*. Shadrach, Meshach, and Abednego had to go into the fiery furnace to be delivered. Daniel spent a night with the lions -- in their den.

So you're wrangling with the devil. That's a good thing. When you don't run headlong into him for weeks at a time, it's usually because you're walking with him. Falling into temptation?

1. Count it all joy. (James 1:1-3)
2. Look for the way of escape. (1 Corinthians 10:13)
3. Submit yourself to God. (James 4:7)
4. Now resist the devil, and he will flee. (James 4:7)

This is a good fight because we win. (2 Timothy 4:7) But it is still a fight, so get in there and contend for the faith. (Jude 1-3) Going through hell? Follow the devil brick road. (Luke 10:19)

You Are (UR) -- being followed.

MARCH 9 *(PSALM 23:1-6)*

Don't look now, but they are right behind you. Don't try to get away. First of all, you can't. And even if you could, you wouldn't want to. The only reason they haven't overtaken you yet is because most of us insist on ripping and running as fast as we can, trying to find what's behind us. Confusing? Think like a biblical bride. Rebekah is a great example. (Genesis 24) Slow down. Take time to help a stranger. (Hebrews 13:1-3) Rest. (Hebrews 4:1-11) Trust. (Proverbs 3:3-6) Get found. (Proverbs 18:22) Still don't know who's after you? Goodness and Mercy. And if you'll continue to follow your shepherd, they will be there all the days of your life.

You Are (UR) -- strong in the Lord.

At the end of the day, the call is to be what you are. *"Finally, my brethren,"* Paul says. He doesn't say get strong. He doesn't even say become strong. *"Be strong,"* he says. But in order to be strong, we must first believe that we are strong.

Nehemiah was on the right track when he admonished the children of Israel. They wept when they heard the word of the Lord. Perhaps an appropriate reaction at times, but not then. He reminded them that *"this day is holy unto our Lord: neither be ye sorry; for the joy of the Lord is your strength."* (Nehemiah 8:8-10)

This was not Nehemiah's first such minder. In chapter four of the same book, he told them: *"Be not ye afraid of them: remember the Lord, which is great and terrible, and fight for your brethren, your sons, and your daughters, your wives, and your houses."* (vs. 14) And therein lies the key to strength.

Remember - Believe - Be

"For whosoever shall call on the name of the Lord shall be saved. How then shall they call on him in whom they have not believed? And how shall they believe in him of whom they have not heard? And how shall they hear without a preacher? And how shall they preach, except they be sent? As it is written, How beautiful are the feet of them that preach the gospel of peace, and bring glad tidings of good things! So then faith cometh by hearing, and hearing by the word of God." (Romans 10:13-15,17)

You have heard the authorized word of God from those who have been commissioned to preach (boldly proclaim) it to you. Now you must believe it in you heart and cry out the call that brings salvation. **Say it out loud!** I am strong in the Lord!

You Are (UR) -- inconsiderate.

MARCH 11 *(ROMANS 4:13-19-25)*

I know that doesn't sound very encouraging, but consider this. Some things just don't deserve our consideration. Lies that present themselves as facts. (Romans 3:4) Fools that misrepresent themselves as wise. (Romans 1:18-22) And anything else, including the devil himself, that would dare to exalt itself against the knowledge of God. (2 Corinthians 10:3-5)

The things that tend to vie most ardently for your consideration are the things/people that are closest to you, your own body and your loved ones topping the list. **Remember:** It was Eve's consideration for the devil's opinion and Adam's consideration for Eve's feelings that got us where we are today. Will people call you inconsiderate when you obey God rather than them? Certainly. But have you considered that it is far less important *what* they call you than it is *how* they call you? Long distance in heaven, or local in hell. (Luke 16:19-26)

Are (UR) -- a child of God.

MARCH 12 *(ROMANS 8:14)*

Some would say we all are, but the scriptures just don't agree. And that distinction is a very powerful one. (John 1:12,13) When the *"prodigal"* son returned to his father's house, he was furnished with shoes to prove he was a son rather than a servant. The ring that he was given was a seal of witness that he was, in fact, who he said he was and it gave him legal access to all that his father had. In effect, he was given access to a new inheritance after having squandered the first one. Your footwear is the preparation of the gospel of peace. (Ephesians 6:14-16) Your ring of witness is the Holy Spirit. (2 Corinthians 1:22) Others may sing it, but you can prove that you are a child of God with full rights and privileges to a glorious inheritance -- now.

You Are (UR) -- the salt of the earth.

(Matthew 5:13) MARCH 13

Ever wonder why spices cost so much? Five bucks for a little jar of Tarragon -- Whew! There was a time when they were actually used as money *(forms of exchange)*. The reason is relatively simple. They were the primary means of food preservation prior to refrigeration. Salt and pepper were the ones most used. Salt for its strength of preservation. Pepper for its pungent odor. In essence, they made meat rot slower and smell better while it did. Hence -- Salt Pork, Pepper Steak, Pickled Herring, Corned Beef, etc.... The hotter the climate, the more spices people used. That's why food tends to be bland in England and smoking in the Caribbean. (Romans 5:20,21) I'm sure you've noticed that things are heating up and the world stinks worse than ever. Flesh is going bad faster and faster. Which means, your value is increasing each day -- Salty.

You Are (UR) -- highly favored.

(Luke 1:26-29) MARCH 14

That's what the angel Gabriel told Mary, the mother of Jesus, just before he announced the birth of our Lord. The scriptures go on to say that Mary was troubled at the saying and *"cast in her mind, what manner of salutation this should be."* In 21st Century English you might say she thought: *"What do you mean God likes me?"* Weird isn't it? God loves you and me and He wants to bless our socks off, yet we stagger at the possibility. (Romans 4:19-21) But Mary didn't stagger long. She asked one question -- *"How? I am still a virgin."* (Loose translation) Gabriel explained that the Holy Ghost would be involved. He told that her cousin Elisabeth (another impossible case) was having a similar experience. And then he reminded her of that which we must never forget. *"For with God nothing shall be impossible."* Mary said, *"Hit me."* (Looser translation;-) What will you say -- Oh favored one?

You Are (UR) -- F.R.E.E.

MARCH 15 *(JOHN 8:31-36)*

When the youngest of two sons *(you call him the prodigal)* found himself broke and broken, in a pig sty miles from the heart and home of his father, he also found himself bound. He was bound by a spirit of condemnation that persuaded him to return ashamed and beaten. In his heart, he was nothing more than a slave, worthy only of food to live on and a dead-end job. (Luke 15:11-22) But the love of his father set him **F.R.E.E.**

"When he was a great way off, his father saw him, and had compassion, and ran, and fell on his neck, and kissed him." He **FORGAVE** him. Many of us have returned from failure to a form of "forgiveness" that rendered us suspect, second class citizens in places we once called home. But this son's father went further.

After hearing his son declare his unworthy concept of himself, the father *"said to his servant. 'Bring forth the best robe, and put it on him.'"* He didn't try to clean him up first. He covered him so that no one need see the filth and frailty his error had brought upon him. In one graceful motion he **REDEEMED** and began to **RESTORE** him.

Now our father **EMPOWERS** us. He places the shoes of a son on our feet -- the preparation of the gospel of peace (Ephesians 6:15) -- so that there is no mistaking *(for others or for us)* that we are, indeed, sons.

And finally, he **EXPECTS** us to begin a productive new life. When the "prodigal" son's father placed that ring on his finger, it was a statement of expectation. It was a vote of confidence. It was his way of saying, *"I know you are a prodigy. You are my talented, gifted, prodigious son. You carry my blood in your veins and my spirit in your heart. The creativity, faith, confidence, zeal, and savvy you displayed in gathering that first fortune were qualities I instilled in you. Now I place the authorization for full access to all my resources in and on your hand **(the Holy Spirit is the engagement ring Jesus gives us)** that you may go and build a new inheritance for you and your children's children."*

Father has great expectation for us too. He has set us **F.R.E.E.** We are **Forgiven**. We are **Redeemed** and being **Restored**. We are **Empowered**. And a great **Expectation** is set before us. (Jeremiah 29:11)

You Are (UR) -- a ready writer.

(PSALM 45:1) MARCH 16

The Library of Congress may not house your volumes. Your name may never appear on the New York Times best seller list. But your vision is being written every single day on the fleshy tables of men's hearts. (2 Corinthians 3:1-3) Your tongue is your pen. Tame it! (James 3:1-13) Write your vision plainly that he that reads it may run. (Habakkuk 2:2-4) And one day, when you least expect it; one day when you need it most, that vision is going to speak.

That vision is going to speak to you as a writer. Your son or daughter, a student or subordinate, your spouse or neighbor, or maybe the vagrant you encouraged to try again -- will speak. Your written vision will speak and cause you to run again. So write writer! Write what you have found as touching the king. (Ecclesiastes 12:10-12) It has been said that leaders read and readers lead. If that is so -- Writers rule the world.

You Are (UR) -- a disciple whom Jesus loves.

(JOHN 21:20-23) MARCH 17

That's what the disciples of Jesus called John. If you read Peter's comment in verse 21, it almost sounds as if they were a bit envious of John's relationship with the Lord. Could John have been Jesus' "pet"? **Remember:** God is no respecter of persons. Yes, John was Jesus' pet. And so were all the other disciples. And so are you. What's odd is that we so desperately desire to be accepted by our peers that the devil will tempt us to shun such monickers and even try to do things that distance us from he who genuinely loves us. So say it with me: Yes -- Jesus loves me! The Bible tells me so.

You Are (UR) -- absolutely alive.

MARCH 18 *(JOHN 10:10)*

Dr. Seuss, legendary children's book author and illustrator, had a life that you won't find displayed in the toddlers' section. You could say,

There are some 'other' cats
who wear no hats
that deal with what people try to drown in vats.

One example that I find quite insightful is about death. With his trademark brand of whimsical art he portrays a person in a casket who is quoted as saying: *"I would love to come to the party, but I am absolutely dead."*

When I first read it, I thought, If I should pass away before the Lord returns, that's what I want read to those who gather to celebrate my life. *"Sing, Shout, Eat, Dance, Remember, and Rejoice. Some of you I haven't seen for many years, but thanks for coming to pay your respects. I would love to come to the party but...."* And then the Lord reminded me. Cessation notwithstanding: Death is no longer a part of my resumé. I did it once and lived through it. I will be at the real party -- because I am absolutely alive. (John 11:25,26 / Galatians 2:20/Ephesians 2:1)

You Are (UR) -- confused.

MARCH 19 *(2 CORINTHIANS 4:8)*

Admit it. You don't know what to do. You don't know where you're going. You're scratching your head wondering: *"What just happened?"* You may have your boss fooled. You maintain appearances for your spouse and your kids. But the truth is there are situations about which they don't have a clue either. The encouraging thing is, confused *(perplexed)* as you may be -- you are not hopeless. Even though your head is at a loss for informed answers, your heart assures you: *'All is well.'* Believe it. That peace you feel is supposed to be unexplainable. (Philippians 4:6) Confusing isn't it?

You Are (UR) -- worshipping His Majesty.

(MATTHEW 21:1-9) MARCH 20

When Jesus rode into Jerusalem sitting upon an ass, and a colt the foal of an ass, the people cried, saying, *"Hosanna to the son of David: Blessed is he that cometh in the name of the Lord; Hosanna in the highest."* These same people later cried *"Let him be crucified."* It really doesn't matter, though, what people cry. Jesus remains the King of kings and the Lord of lords. Regardless of our circumstances or others' opinions, we are worshipping His Majesty.

You Are (UR) -- just perfect.

(GENESIS 6:8,9) MARCH 21

Well, provided you are born again, you are just-ified. And that is the highest form of perfection available to you in this life. Noah was called just and perfect in his day and he wasn't even born again. He did exactly what we are doing. He walked with God. Jesus of Nazareth went about doing good and healing all that were oppressed of the devil -- for God was with him. (Acts 10:38) Enoch was translated and did not see death. He was *"not found"* because he walked, by faith, and pleased God. (Hebrews 11:5)

The just live by faith. Habakkuk prophesied it and Paul reaffirmed it. (Habakkuk 2:4 / Romans 1:16,17) That same Paul reminded us *(as many as be perfect)* in his letter to the Philippians, to *"forget those things which are behind and reach forth unto those things which are before and press toward the mark for the prize of the high calling in Christ Jesus."* (Philippians 3:13-15) So, let those that must find fault do as they may. But know in your heart that we who walk with God by faith are just perfect. And if anything is not as it should be -- God will let us know.

You Are (UR) -- an ambassador.

MARCH 22 *(2 CORINTHIANS 5:20,21)*

You represent the interests of heaven in the earth. One great privilege of your charge is that you have diplomatic immunity. The laws of heaven override the laws of earth. (Romans 8:1,2) Now, don't go speeding to work or robbing any banks. The laws of heaven require obedience to the laws of man and authorize human officers to execute judgement on God's behalf. (Romans 13) But condemnation for sin, sickness and disease, poverty and lack, and the rest of life's calamities have no authority over you. Exercise your diplomatic immunity as you represent heaven in Christ's stead.

You Are (UR) -- admitted.

MARCH 23 *(EPHESIANS 2:11-19)*

I played in bands most of my young adult life. Nothing major, mostly hole in the wall, juke joints, on weekends, for little or no money. That notwithstanding, there was something very special about walking into the club and saying: *"I'm with the band."* We weren't quite big enough to have Security, and *"All Access Backstage Passes,"* laminated and hanging around our necks on florescent cord.

But even non-musician friends who accompanied us walked a little taller as they uttered those words. *"I'm with the band."* It evoked a sense of privilege and belonging. I'm sure there was more than a little pride involved. There was also a comfort in knowing that our gifts had made room for us. (Proverbs 18:16)

Now, I'm with Jesus. He's the star. We're his friends. And we have an *"All Access Pass"* into the grace of God. (Romans 5:1,2)

You Are (UR) -- all in the family.

(EPHESIANS 3:14,15) MARCH 24

Family is an important mainstay to life, that is not always immediately accessible. In a world filled with distance, deviants, D.I.N.K.s *(Double Incomes No Kids)* and divorcees, the concept of family can get terribly confused. But you are all *(those who are born again by the power of the Spirit)* in the family of God. It is a "whole family." From Adam to Abraham to Jesus to John. From the heartland to the hinterlands to Hell's Kitchen to Heaven. You may not know them all by name. You may not be able to see or hear them in the natural. But they are there, at all times, praying for and cheering on your victorious walk with God, our Father. (Hebrews 12:1)

Choosing Christ may have strained a natural relationship or two. But something far greater is promised. *"Verily I say unto you, There is no man that hath left house, or brethren, or sisters, or father, or mother, or wife or children, or lands, for my sake, and the gospels, But he shall receive an hundredfold now in this time, houses, and brethren, and sisters, and mothers, and children and lands, with persecutions; and in the world to come eternal life."* (Mark 10:29,30) Archies and Ediths and "Meat Heads" too -- we are all in the family.

You Are (UR) -- between a rock and a hard place.

(MATTHEW 27:57-66) MARCH 25

Jesus's trials were not over when he gave up the ghost. His work on earth was finished, but his work under the earth had just begun. They took him off the cross and sealed him in the tomb. From there, he was on his way to hell. For three days and three nights he dealt with the devil and led captivity captive that we might have victory over death. So the next time you feel like you're between a rock and a hard place, remember: *"You have not yet resisted unto blood, striving against sin."* Look for the *"way of escape,"* and never forget: on the third day, the stone was rolled away.

You Are (UR) -- second.

MARCH 26 *(LUKE 10:25-27)*

It is critical that you know where you are in the *"pecking order."* You should always be second. God IS first. (Exodus 20:1/Matthew 6:33) Some people consider it noble to put others before themselves, but that can become frustrating - fast. We are commanded to love others *as* ourselves. The "Golden Rule" instructs us to do unto others *as* we would have them do unto us. Men are expected to love their wives *as* their own bodies. (Ephesians 5:28) And the apostle Paul encouraged the church at Philippi to esteem others *better than* themselves. If we are to comply with any of the above, we must first consider God, to get the true measure of ourselves, then we will know how to deal with the world.

You Are (UR) -- crucified with Christ.

MARCH 27 *(GALATIANS 2:20,21)*

"Were you there when they crucified my Lord?"

I always took the words to this popular spritual with the proverbial grain of salt. My savior's passion took place over two thousand years ago. How could I have been there? Then I read Paul's letter to the saints at Galatia and reconsidered my own experienc with the Alpha and Omega, the beginning and the ending, the God who was and is and is to come.

Surely we have escaped the limitations of time and space. Just as the law of sin and death have lost their grip to the law of the Spirit of life in Christ Jesus, so likewise, we have caught hold on the victory Jesus won on the cross.

Say it out loud! *"I am crucified with Christ: nevertheless I live; yet not I, but Christ liveth in me: and the life which I now live in the flesh I live by the Son of God, who loved me, and gave himself for me."*

You Are (UR) -- sanctified.

(1 Corinthians 1:1-3) MARCH 28

I spent a lot of summers with my grandmother as a child. Every so often, she would make a pound cake. You knew pound cake was on the menu, as soon as you walked into the kitchen, by one unmistakable sign. There would be four sticks of butter in a covered glass dish, waiting patiently as they softened, on the hot water heater. That butter was not for toast, pancakes or grits.

If grandma found crumbs in that butter, you got spanked and you didn't get any pound cake either. That butter was sanctified -- set apart -- for pound cake. God set you apart to make something out of you too. Be patient. Soften up. And stay away from mischievous eight year olds with promises of toast and pancakes, 'cause -- like grandma -- God won't use crumby butter.

You Are (UR) -- well taken care of.

(1 Peter 5:6,7) MARCH 29

Say It -- Out Loud! I am well taken care of. It is a joy to submit myself completely to the God of all creation, because I know He cares for me. He will never leave me nor forsake me. (Hebrews 13:5) He meets all of my need: Not according to my level of education, accomplishment or pay, but according to His riches in glory, by Christ Jesus. (Philippians 4:19)

I don't have to be careful for anything. I can talk to God, make specific requests, and then say thank you, (Philippians 4:6) because I am confident that I receive the things that I desire when I pray and I know that I shall have them because my heart is aligned with God's will. (Mark 11:22,23/1 John 5:14-16) My heart is well kept with the peace of God from the God of peace. (Philippians 4:7/Hebrews 13:20,21) I am well taken care of.

You Are (UR) -- well equipped to handle fear.

MARCH 30 *(PROVERBS 3:25,26)*

Say It -- Out Loud! I am well equipped to handle fear. Dismal circumstances may come at me at dizzying speeds, but that's okay. I don't have to be afraid. I will not fear, because I know some things. (James 1:1-2-4) I know there will be trials of my faith. I also know how to set myself and patiently seek the Lord. (2 Chronicles 20:1-1-3) I know that if I seek Him, I shall find Him. (Proverbs 8:17) Therefore, I know that I can count it all joy because in His presence, there is fulness of joy and at His right hand there are pleasures forevermore. (Psalm 16:11)

I know that He will never leave me nor forsake me. (Hebrews 13:5,6) He is my helper and I need not fear what man shall do unto me. God is for me. No one and no thing can successfully stand against me. (Romans 8:31) The Lord is my light and my salvation; whom shall I fear? The Lord is the strength of my life; of whom shall I be afraid? (Psalm 27:1) I am bold as a lion. I will not flee like the wicked. (Proverbs 28:1) I am righteous. I am set. I am free. I am well equipped to handle fear.

You Are (UR) -- Abraham's seed.

MARCH 31 *(GALATIANS 3:13-29)*

Say It -- Out Loud! I am Abraham's seed. I am an heir, according to God's promise. God chose me. I certainly didn't choose Him. (John 15:16) I used to be dead in trespasses and sins, but because of His mercy, I am no longer far away, outside the covenants of promise, without hope, and without God in the world. (Ephesians 2:11-22) I am made nigh (drawn close) by the blood of Christ. The wall is broken down. No more Jew or Gentile. No more enmity (anger that is willing to kill). I am part of the one new man. It's good to be a fellow citizen with the saints and of the household of God. It's good to be fitly framed together for an habitation of God through the Spirit. I am Abraham's seed.

You Are (UR) -- nobody's fool.

(1 CORINTHIANS 15:12-20) APRIL 1

I realize that I've used this heading before. But who was thinking about April Fool's day in February? Don't answer that;-) Here's a different take on the same truth.

The fool hath said in his heart, there is no God. (Psalm 14:1) Let's say, for conversation's sake, the fools are right. Believing in a 'non-existent' God, give or take a little restraint, makes life better and the fool just winds up with nowhere to go. But imagine the horror of having lived an unrestrained life without obedience to God and finding that He is alive and well. Even a fool can figure this one out. But hey! You're nobody's fool.

You Are (UR) -- anointed.

(2 CORINTHIANS 1:21,22) APRIL 2

Before you puff up or blow it off, make sure you understand what's happening. It's easy to juxtapose anointed with powerful, like every rooster must believe that his crowing makes the sun come up. After all, both groups of elements do tend to show up at about the same time. But it's very dangerous to confuse the cause with the effect.

Yes, you are anointed. You are drenched, soaked, covered, saturated, infused, dripping, drowning in, oozing with, the glory of our great God. (Psalm 133) But that's someone else's coat you're wearing. It's a nice coat. But it's not yours. (2 Kings 2) Walk tall when you put it on, but get used to being known as the one who pours water over His hands. (2 Kings 3:11) Go everywhere. Do good. Heal all that are oppressed of the devil. Just remember: God is with you. And you are covered. (Acts 10:38) **Say It Loud!** I am anointed.

You Are (UR) -- God's workmanship.

APRIL 3 *(EPHESIANS 2:8-10)*

When God formed Adam of the dust of the ground, He wasn't creating on the fly -- just seeing what He might come up with. He had already mapped out this new creation and designed a destiny for him throughout eternity. And you were in the plans. You are the work of God's hands. He will never forsake you and He is determined to fashion you to perfection (Psalm 138:8) You may not be sure of anything else, but be confident of this very thing: He isn't going to quit until "the day of Jesus Christ." (Philippians 1:6)

Though there is a need for constant examination and adjustment, (1 Corinthians 11:28-32) He knows not to judge (condemn) the work before the time. (1 Corinthians 4:1-5) And He has already prepared good works for you to walk into. He instructs you to *"work out your salvation with fear and trembling."* (Philippians 2:12,13) And it is Him at work in you both to will (dream) and to do (perform) of His good pleasure. **Say It Loud!** I am God's workmanship, and this thing is working!

You Are (UR) -- delightful.

APRIL 4 *(PSALM 1)*

(See Also Micah 7:18) Your life is filled with delight. On good days, your delight is in the law of the Lord. You worship Him. You praise Him. You love Him with all your heart, all your mind, all your strength, and all your soul. You love your neighbor as yourself. It's delightful. On the rare days when you forget any or all of the above -- He delights in mercy. Confess your sins and he is faithful to forgive. (1John 1:9) Confess your faults and be healed. (James 5:16) The world may seem a bit dark and dismal, but you are walking in -- delight;-)

You Are (UR) -- born again.

(JOHN 3:1-7) APRIL 5

Nicodemus found it incredible. *"How can a man be born when he is old?"* He said to Jesus. *"Can he enter the second time into his mother's womb, and be born?"* Some people try. When life gets overwhelming, they curl up into the fetal position and wait for the storm to pass. But not you. You are born again. You are born of the Spirit and of the water. You have received power to become a child of God. (John 1:12)

You are part of the family, with relatives in heaven and earth. (Ephesians 3:15) You think your mother's birthday parties were grand? When you were born again, all of heaven rejoiced. (Luke 15:7) There are people all over this world ruing the day they were born? Fighting the fact that they were born on the *"wrong side of the tracks"*? But you beat all of that, when you got -- **Say It Loud!** -- Born Again!

You Are (UR) -- holding the truth.

(ROMANS 1:18-20) APRIL 6

*"People pay for the lives they lead and the crimes they commit
and the blood-guiltiness from which they flee, whether they know it or not. <u>The
effort not to know what one knows is the most corrupting effort one can make.</u>
But the anguish which comes when the buried knowledge begins to force itself
to the light...has driven countless thousands to madness or murder or grace."*

James Baldwin -- 1966
(Underline mine.)

See Romans 14:11,12 / 2 Peter 3:1-9 esp. vs. 5 / Luke 12:1-3 And
consider Nebudchadnezzar, Judas, Cain, David and Paul,
who, like you, also held the truth.

You Are (UR) -- your brother's keeper.

APRIL 7 *(GENESIS 4)*

Cain had the dubious distinction of being the first born of fallen man. Born to shed the blood of animal sacrifices. Born to till the ground of a cursed earth that would resist every effort with thorns and thistles. Born to bring his mother the world's first labor pains. It is no cliché: Cain's was a life of literal blood, sweat and tears. And then came baby brother.

Suddenly Cain had a playmate -- a friend. He also had a source of comparison and competition. Can you say sibling rivalry? Abel was destined and some might say doomed, to be the source and object of his brother's frustration. The scriptures don't say how old the boys were when the *"incident"* occurred. *"In the process of time it came to pass,"* we are told. But time, as it was with their father Adam, is a formidable proving ground for relationships with God and man.

Hebrews declares that it was faith that made Abel's sacrifice *"more excellent"* than Cain's. Verse four declares that his faith obtained him a righteous witness and more importantly, a voice after death -- something akin to eternal life. But what did he do that was so different from Cain? He believed God and did what God said. The evidence is in the blood.

Abel was a keeper of sheep. He offered *"the firstlings of his flock and...the fat thereof."* (Genesis 4:4) But in order for Cain, *"a tiller of the ground,"* to offer an acceptable sacrifice -- a blood sacrifice -- he would have had to get it, yet another year, from baby brother. And therein lies the rub.

Time had taken its toll. Year after year of needing the gifts of another to please God and maybe even to please Adam, had come to a blood curdling climax. So when God asked; *"Where is Abel thy brother?"* Cain's *"Am I my brother's keeper?,"* erupted from a place far beneath the surface. The rich young ruler struggled with the same concept. *"And who is my neighbor?"* (Luke 10:25-29) Such questions seem to characterize strained relationships.

You Are (UR) -- your brother's keeper.

God is not ambiguous in his answer to Cain's question. Your neighbor -- your brother -- is the earthly object of your love. He is to be loved as you love yourself, second only to me, God says. And while we are trying to justify ourselves, God has questions of his own. *"How can a man say he loves God whom he can't see and hate his brother whom he sees every-day?"* (1 John 4:7-21) How indeed?

At the end of the day, because Cain couldn't live with his brother, he killed his brother. And God made his labor even harder and estranged him from all of humanity. Ironically, Cain knew that this first murder could potentially be the catalyst for another -- his own. So he, like David, Hezekiah, and Jabez, petitioned God. *"My punishment is greater than I can bear."* And Cain experienced the mercy of God that causes the rain to fall on the wicked and the just and the sun to shine on the evil and the Good. God marked him with a seal of compassionate protection.

Cain went on to build a city east of Eden. Quite an accomplishment for any man. There don't appear to be any further altercations in his life. He married and fathered a son -- Enoch *(not the one that walked with God and was "not found")*. That notwithstanding, he is remembered as a son of Belial who slew his brother. (1 John 3:11,12 / Jude 5-16 esp. vs 11)

It continually amazes me how one rash thought -- one action in anger -- can alter the course of an entire life. Solomon understood it and so should you: *"He that is slow to anger is better than the mighty; and he that ruleth his spirit than he that taketh (**or buildeth**) a city."* (Proverbs 16:32) Remember: You are your brother's keeper.

"One man with courage makes a majority."

Andrew Jackson

You Are (UR) -- worthy.

APRIL 9 *(ACTS 5:1-42)*

(esp. vs. 41) I know you have heard, maybe even prayed, thousands of pious prayers proclaiming your unworthiness in an attempt to sound or be humble. Now you can experience true humility and rejoice in the fact that you are worthy. You are worthy to suffer shame for His name.

Be an irritation to the devil and his cohorts. When they show up -- cast them out. When they try to shut you up -- you preach louder. When they lock you up -- praise God, because you are free even in bondage. When they threaten to kill you -- know that *"to live is Christ, and to die (for Him) is gain."* (Philippians 1:21) Surely your bold proclamation of the cross of Christ cuts to the heart. You are worthy, because He is worthy. You are worthy to suffer shame for His name.

You Are (UR) -- a good soldier.

APRIL 10 *(2 TIMOTHY 2:1-4)*

In this age of watching wars on television, it's difficult not to get caught up in the play by play coverage of this most curious of human conflicts. Wars, like the poor, it seems, we will have with us always. (Matthew 24:1-14/Mark 14:1-7) So pray for our leaders and encourage our troops, and never forget that the critical battle is waged in an arena that neither tanks, ships, nor aircraft can breach. The true battle is in the heavens.

> *"For we wrestle not against flesh and blood, but against principali-*
> *ties, against powers, aaginst spiritual wickedness in high places."*
> (Ephesians 6:10-20)

Be a faithful soldier. Don't get entangled in the temporary war that is seen. (2 Corinthians 4:15-18) Rule your own spirit and the strongholds of the world will be no problem. (Proverbs 16:32)

You Are (UR) -- a natural.

(2 PETER 1:1-4) APRIL 11

Say it out loud! I have the nature of God. I have been born again to an inheritance incorruptible and undefiled, that doesn't fade away, reserved in heaven for me. (1 Peter 1:1-4) Grace and peace are increasingly multiplied unto me as I increase in the knowledge of my father and of His son, my savior and brother, Jesus Christ. He wishes above all things that I prosper and be in health even as my soul prospers. (3 John 2) And to make sure I get it, He restores my soul. (Psalm 23)

I shall not want! God makes me lie down in abundance. I am being led daily to places of peace. He keeps me from evil to protect his name. I will not fear. That's not my nature. I inherited the Spirit of power and of love and of a sound mind. (2 Timothy 1:7) I eat well and I have more than enough. I am continually followed - covered - protected by goodness and mercy. And one day soon, I am going home to a place prepared especially for me. I'm in Him and that's His nature.

You Are (UR) -- God's people.

(1 PETER 2:9-10) APRIL 12

Say it loud! I'm God's and I'm proud! (Psalm 44:8) He chose me. He ordained me to proclaim His kingdom. (John 15:16) He made me holy by his blood. I am special to him and he has a pointed purpose for me. (Jeremiah 29:11)

I'm going to praise him. I'm going to talk wonderfully about him to everyone I meet. Because he called me out of darkness and now I walk in his light. What I used to be proud of was nothing to him. (Philippians 3:4-7) But now, I am God's people and that is something to shout about.

You Are (UR) -- worthy of your meat.

APRIL 13 *(MATTHEW 10:1-14)*

Times are tough. The economy's down. C'est le guerre. (It's the war.) Money is tighter than it's ever been. Wait! Don't I remember Marvin Gaye singing that line thirty years ago? Well, somebody's lying. My God says He will supply all your need. Not according to the economy. Not according to how goes the war. My God shall supply all your need according to His riches in glory by Christ Jesus. (Philippian 4:19) But here's what He told me yesterday.

> *"What you have will always be a function of how much you believe there is and how much of it you believe you are worth."*

Jacob got it. Laban knew it. (Genesis 31:27) The "prodigal" son got it. His big brother hated it. (Luke 15:11-32) We'd better get it, no matter who hates it. It's not the economy. It's certainly not the war. It's the devil and he's a liar. There is more than enough and you are worthy of your meat.

You Are (UR) -- justified.

APRIL 14 *(ROMANS 5:1-9)*

Say it! I am justified. I am made right. Not by works of righteousness which I have done. (Titus 3:3-7) I was not right. I was wrong. Wrong as two left shoes. But God loved me and He sent Jesus to die for me. I confessed my sins, and He was faithful and just to forgive me my sins and cleanse me from all unrighteousness. (1 John 1:9) Now I stand in His righteousness. He has made me right. I am Justified -- Just as if I'd never done anything.

You Are (UR) -- a taxpayer.

(MATTHEW 17:24-27) APRIL 15

Today is filing day for federal income taxes, and folk are scrambling to make the deadline. In the midst of the scramble, some may be wondering (pronounced grumbling) why we have to pay so much and maybe even how they're going to pay. But Jesus made it clear in the original "Show me the money!" speech. (Matthew 22:15-21) *"Give Caesar what is Caesar's and give God what is God's."* There should be such a scramble to pay tithes and offerings. But there is power in Jesus' logic.

The standard declaration of privilege in this country is: "Hey! I'm a taxpayer." Thank God we have the comfort of knowing that there's a fish, somewhere, with Caesar's money in his mouth. If it's any further consolation, had Caesar Augustus not levied taxes on the world two millennia ago, we'd be singing "Oh Little Town of Nazareth" at Christmas. So the next time the devil infringes on your rights, remind him: Hey! I'm a tax (tithe) payer.

You Are (UR) -- in for a surprise.

(1 CORINTHIANS 2:9,10) APRIL 16

Don't look now, but there are great things gathering around you. Actually, you can look all you want, your eyes won't focus on them anyway until you believe what God has said about you. He's not lying. He can't lie. You are blessed. You are healed. Your needs are met. You do have the victory. Your enemies will flee. And God doesn't need your help to fight them off. If it were not so, He would have told you. (John 14:1,2) **STOP!** Do like Jehoshaphat -- set yourself *(set your heart to seek the Lord)*, stand still, and see the salvation of the Lord. If you keep trying to work it out, good will come, but you won't see it. (Jeremiah 17:5-8) Let the Spirit of God lead you and you will see.

You Are (UR) -- being talked about.

APRIL 17 *(ROMANS 1:8-12)*

I know I talk about you, just about everyday. I talk to God about you and I ask Him to bless you and strengthen you and reveal himself to you. Some of you I mention by name. And when I hear from you, I tell others about what God is doing in your lives. I thank God for each opportunity to speak to you by e-mail, on the phone, one-on-one, and in churches across the country. Your faith strengthens my faith and I pray that my faith strengthens yours. Now, that's worth talking about.

You Are (UR) -- beyond words.

APRIL 18 *(2 CORINTHIANS 9:15)*

(1 Peter 1:3-9) Some people don't talk about religion. Others are the butt of every joke because of their religion. But you have a relationship that is beyond words. People don't know what to say about you. Even Jesus asked: *"Whom do men say that I the Son of man am?"* Outsiders had varying opinions. Insiders were silent. It took a revelation to get to the truth. (Matthew 16: 13-17)

Speechless. That's how your love for Jesus leaves onlookers. They don't understand it. They can't describe it. They won't acknowledge their need for it. But they certainly want it. That's why you must rely on the Holy Spirit to enable you to answer every man who asks you about the hope that you have. (1 Peter 3:13-16)

Sinners don't talk about their gods because there is not that much to say. They snicker at others' "fanaticism" because it is often laughable. But the love of God that is manifest toward, in and through you is - no - you are beyond words.

You Are (UR) -- too quick to judge.

(1 CORINTHIANS 4:3-5) APRIL 19

Yogi Bera said: *"It ain't over 'til it's over."* And Jack Webb only wanted: *"The facts maam, just the facts."* But maybe Jack Nicholson was right. *"You can't handle the truth."*

Well, Jesus is the way, the truth, and the life, and he says, examine yourself, (1 Corinthians 11:28) but let me decide what ought to happen to you. (Acts 1:7/Hebrews 10:30) Meanwhile, like the woman taken in adultery, there's nobody on the planet fit to condemn you *(and that includes you)* and neither does Jesus, so go and sin no more. (John 8:3-11)

You Are (UR) -- a true worshipper.

(JOHN 4:21-24) APRIL 20

Jesus is coming. The question is: When? Answer: In an hour. That's right. In a day and an hour that you know not. (Matthew 24:36-46) So for all practical purposes, the hour is now. Now is the appointed time. Today is the day of salvation. (2 Corinthians 6:1,2) The hour cometh, and now is when the true worshippers shall worship the Father in spirit and in truth. And you are a true worshipper.

You are a true worshipper -- all the time -- everywhere. Sure, we gather together. Yes, we honor the sabbath. And we do so more and more, as we see the day approaching. (Hebrews 10:19-25) But between our gatherings, all of heaven rejoices. (Luke 15:10) Each day, we are compassed about by a great cloud of witnesses. (Hebrews 12:1,2) His mercies are renewed every morning. And He daily loads us with benefits. (Psalm 68:19) Worship Him. Give Him glory and honor. He is worthy. The hour cometh, and now is when the true worshippers shall worship the Father in spirit and in truth. And you are a true worshipper.

You Are (UR) -- following a pattern.

APRIL 21 *(TITUS 2:6-8)*

God came into the garden after Adam and Eve ate of the tree of the knowledge of good and evil, asking questions. Where are you? Who told you that? And what have you done? He did the same thing to Cain prior to and after his murderous transgression. Why are you mad? What's wrong with your face? Where is your brother? And what have you done? In case you haven't noticed, there is a pattern here.

Relationship affects Perception
Perception drives Action

The pattern never changes. Where you are in relationship to God and man will affect who and what you believe, which will determine how you see and feel about yourself, which drives you to do what you do.

You Are (UR) -- a troublemaker.

APRIL 22 *(1 KINGS 18:17,18)*

At least, that's what the world would like to believe. They have convinced themselves that your "religious fanaticism" is the cause of most of the world's evils. Wars, conflicts, intolerance, etc.... It's all your fault.

If it were not for your disdain, they could sin without guilt or restraint. (2 Thessalonians 2:5-7) Your antiquated, backwards values run contrary to their progressive 21st century desires. (Acts 17:6) Admit it. You are one of them. Aren't you? Don't deny it. (Matthew 26:69-75) You are one of them who have turned the world upside down. (Acts 17:5-9)

You Are (UR) -- not matching your background.

(JEREMIAH 13:22-27) APRIL 23

In his short story **"How The Leopard Got His Spots,"** Rudyard Kipling tells a tale of adaptation. It seems the Leopard and the Ethiopian were starving to death because the rest of the animals left the High Veldt for the shadows of the forest. The then sandy-yellow-brownish Leopard and Ethiopian were driven, by their hunger, to follow. Soon they were faced with the seeming invisibility of their formerly easy prey, and more importantly, the glaring obviousness of their inability to blend in. This promted the Ethiopian to enlighten the angry leopard with these telling words: *"The long and little of it is that we don't match our backgrounds."* He spoke of camouflage. I speak of heritage. Either way, the conspicuous offender tends to go hungry.

You Are (UR) -- strong.

(JOEL 3:9,10) APRIL 24

Say it! I am strong! The joy of the Lord is my strength. (Nehemiah 8:8-10) Sometimes people faint in the day of adversity because their strength is small. (Proverbs 24:10) But I can renew my strength. (Isaiah 40:28-31) I can build up myself on my most holy faith, praying in the Holy Ghost. (Jude 20) I don't have to stagger at the promises of God. I can be strong in faith - fully persuaded that what God has promised, He is also able to perform. (Romans 4:19-21)

I can be strengthened with might by His Spirit in my inner man. (Ephesians 3:14-21) I can receive strength, like Sarah, to conceive the seed of the word. I can say, like Mary, *"be it unto me according to thy word,"* because I judge Him faithful who promised. (Hebrews 11:11/Luke 1:26-38) I am strong. I can bear the infirmities of the weak, because I am strong. (Romans 15:1,2) I am very strong and courageous. I will not stumble or be dismayed. (Joshua 1:6-8) I have not fainted, but believe to see the goodness of the Lord in the land of the living and he has strengthened my heart. (Psalm 27:13,14) I am strong!

You Are (UR) -- in Christ.

APRIL 25 *(2 CORINTHIANS 5:17-21)*

Have you been trying to "find yourself"? You are not in the want ads. You are not on the social calendar. You are not in the funny papers. You are in Christ. You are a new creature. Old things are passed away. All things are become new. And all things are of God. All things are of God. All things are of God! You have been reconciled. Made right. Now that you have found yourself -- relax. The devil can't. Your life is hid with Christ in God. (Colossians 3:1-3) And now that we have told him where you are, he still doesn't dare come after you. Why? You are in Christ.

You Are (UR) -- changing.

APRIL 26 *(2 CORINTHIANS 4:16)*

(1 Corinthians 15:51) There are days when I wonder if I will ever change. (Jeremiah 13:22,23) Then it hits me. I am changing. I never cared about changing before. Sure, my flesh is resisting. The sin that dwells in me is warring against my mind. (Romans 7) It gets frustrating sometimes. It is uncanny how easily I can be set upon. (Hebrews 12:1,2) But there is joy and hope even in the frustration.

I am changing. I am fighting the good fight of faith. I am resisting the devil and he is fleeing. And I know that it is Jesus who shall deliver me from the body of this death. Outwardly, I perish, but inwardly, I am being renewed (changed) day by day. And one day soon, I shall be changed completely and irrevocably. In a moment. In a twinkling of an eye. Thank you Lord. I am changing.

You Are (UR) -- going to see the King.

Soon and very soon, - we are going to see the King. André Crouch wrote it years ago, and it is still true. On earth and throughout eternity, the same quality will bring you before kings. **Diligence:** *Faithful personal attention and close continuous application and effort.* Faithful work will bring you before earthly kings. Works of faith will bring you before the King of kings. And diligence is the common denominator. Because faith without works is dead. (James 2:14-26)

We have all received gifts. (1 Timothy 4:14) Make sure you have the gift of faith. (Ephesians 2:8-10/2 Thessalonians 3:1,2)) To some of us, our gifts are precious. (2 Peter 1:1) But some of us neglect them. Our natural gifts will bring us before great men -- earthly kings, if you will. (Proverbs 18:16) But without faith, it is impossible to please the King of kings. (Hebrews 11:6) Diligence about earthly gifts produces substance -- things. But faith is the substance of things hoped for. (Hebrews 11:1) Whether obtained or hoped for, however, the substance of the diligent man is precious. (Proverbs 12:26,27) So be diligent -- in work and in faith. Because on earth or in heaven -- it is the only way to see the KING.

You Are (UR) -- one of many sons.

Some translations and paraphrases of the Holy Scriptures call Jesus God's *"one and only Son."* This is how they 'clarify' King James' *"only begotten."* (John 1:14) But changing "only begotten" to "one and only" is extremely problematic for us. Do the math. If God has one and only one son, then Peter, Paul, James, and John are all liars and we *"are of all men most miserable."* But just as Mary, the mother of Jesus, went on to have other children by Joseph, (Matthew 13:55) so likewise, God has since fathered many sons and daughters by the Spirit of adoption. (Romans 8:14-17) Praise God. Jesus is the firstborn among many brethren. (Romans 8:29) And you are one of many sons.

You Are (UR) -- always going to win.

APRIL 29 *(1 CORINTHIANS 15:57)*

Say it. Out Loud! I am always going to win. Not by might, nor by power, but by God's Spirit. He said so. (Zechariah 4:6) He always causes me to triumph in Christ Jesus. And through Christ, He gives me the victory. (2 Corinthians 2:14) It may look like it's over sometimes. But I won't be moved by what I see. I walk by faith and not by sight. (2 Corinthians 5:7) The challenges I face from day to day are but for a moment. They don't know it, but they are working for me. I will not look at them. They are temporary. They are subject to change. My eyes are fixed on the word of God. It is eternal. (2 Corinthians 4:13-18) And it says I win. God is for me. Who can successfully stand against me? (Romans 8:31,32) I won't quit. I won't give up. I won't back down. I won't stop. I am always going to win.

You Are (UR) -- not to fear.

APRIL 30 *(MARK 5:35,36)*

Look at yourself in the mirror and say it. **Out Loud!** Be not afraid, only believe. Be not afraid of sudden fear. (Proverbs 3:25) For God has not given us the spirit of fear, but of power and of love and of a sound mind. (2 Timothy 1:7) I will not let you be troubled heart. Neither will I let you be afraid. I believe in God. I believe in Jesus also. In my Father's house are many mansions. There is provision for all my needs. There is healing from all my diseases. There is forgiveness of all my sins, deliverance from evil and protection from all of life's calamities. **IF IT WERE NOT SO -- HE WOULD HAVE TOLD ME!** (John 14:1,2) Bless the Lord, O my soul: and all that is within me, bless his holy name. Bless the Lord, O my soul, and forget not all his benefits. He redeems my life from destruction and crowns me with loving kindness and tender mercies. He satisfies my mouth with good things: so that my youth is renewed like the eagle's. So bless the Lord O my soul. Be not afraid -- Only believe.

You Are (UR) -- standing in the gap.

(EZEKIEL 22:29,30) MAY 1

On more than one occassion, God has expressed his displeasure with what is going on in the world. In Noah's day, God was so displeased, that He set out to destroy His creation. Had it not been for Noah's righteous unwillingness to conform to the norms of his age, there would be no rainbows. And more importantly, there would be no men to see them.

Noah stood in the gap (the G.A.P.), the same gap that God has called us to stand in. Noah stood in the *"good, acceptable, and perfect will of God,"* (Romans 12:1,2) that can only be proven by those who refuse to conform to this world, but rather are transformed by the renewing of their minds.

Paul begged the Corinthians, and I beg you, *"by the mercies of God, that you present your bodies a living sacrifice, holy, acceptable unto God."* It's really the least we can do. God is always looking for someone. He has found me and you. You are standing in the gap.

You Are (UR) -- de branch. He is de vine.

(JOHN 15:5) MAY 2

So sang Keith Green and it made all the sense in the world. What doesn't make sense is that anyone would unplug and become fruitless. Without the vine you can do nothing. Cut flowers are pretty for a minute, but they soon die. Abide in the vine. Live, dwell, flourish, and grow in Him. Don't be a cast away. You will only wither away. Suck up those nutrients that flow through the vine. Grow fat on the living water that is provided by our father, the husbandman. Bear fruit and you can ask what you will.

"Remember He is de vine, and you are de branch, He'd love to get you through it if you'd give Him a chance. Just keep doing your best, And pray that it's blessed, And Jesus takes care of the rest." **Keith Green**

You Are (UR) -- welcomed.

MAY 3 *(1 THESSALONIANS 5:18)*

That's what my parents used to say to us when we forgot to say thank you. They were trying to teach us to appreciate the things that we, so often, received. We are all the beneficiaries of what I call "Peripheral Blessing" -- things we enjoy in life that we didn't earn. You know, like: everything. (1 Corinthians 4:1-7 esp. vs. 7)

For the most part, mom and dad enjoyed watching us enjoy the fruits of their labor. But every now and then, they would have to reestablish the relationship. Especially on those days when we would blow up at them because we didn't get something we really wanted and/or felt we deserved. On days like that we would huff and puff and express our disappointment. And if we were really full of ourselves we would announce, *"I'm going to my room!"*

Such proclaimations were usually followed by a crisp turn and a slammed door. It upset mom, but dad was always calm. The door would open and he would clarify. *"You don't have a room. You live in a room in my house. And as long as you live in my house, drink my water, eat my food, wear my clothes, ride in my car and breath my air, you will do what I say."*

Daddy owned the air. I think he still does. He would calmly close the door to the room he was letting us sulk in with this loving reminder. *"And by the way -- You're welcomed."* (Philippians 4:6-8/1 Timothy 2:1/1 Timothy 4:4/2 Corinthians 4:13-15)

Every day, people slam the door on God. Sometimes it's because they wanted a sunny day and he sent a rainy one. I always marvel at meteorologists that distinguish the two as good or bad. But God lets us sulk in his world, mercifully allowing the rain to fall on the evil and the good and the sun to shine on the wicked and the just. Not willing that any should perish, he sent his only begotten son to die for a thankless world. And I look forward to hearing him say one day, *"You are welcomed."*

You Are (UR) -- lacking one thing.

Funny how one thing can make all the difference. The rich young ruler appeared to have it made, but he knew he was missing something. *"Good Master, what shall I do that I may inherit eternal life?"* he said. Ahhhh the rich. Most folk would have been satisfied with knowing how to earn it, though neither is possible. (Ephesians 2:8-10)

"One thing thou lackest," Jesus said. That's not too bad. Just one thing away from eternity. But what a thing it is. Blind Bartimaeus understood it. His sight was the one thing between him and happiness. (Mark 10:46-52) Jairus had a daughter. Mary and Martha had a brother. Daniel had a lions' den. Job had his children You may imagine a laundry list at such a time. Just like we are all sure that we would use one of our three wishes to ask for unlimited wishes if the genie ever showed up. But, trust me, there is one thing.

Paul proclaimed, *"this one thing I do."* (Philippians 3:1-14 esp. vs 13) David desired *"one thing"* of the Lord. (Psalm 27:4) This he was committed to *"seek after."* That one thing can cause us to lose sight of everything else. So the right thing must be first. (Matthew 6:33)

The indebted widow said to the prophet, *"thine handmaid hath not anything in the house, save a pot of oil."* Though far from the truth, the Lord used that thing, that pot of oil, to solve her problem. He knew it was the *one thing* she had confidence in. He knew it was the *one thing* she valued.

This is the confidence we have in Him. (1 John 5:14) All things are ours. (1 Corinthians 3:21-23) God has given them unto us. (Romans 8:31,32) But the one thing can cause us not to see them. (2 Kings 6:8-17/Jeremiah 17:5-9) The one thing can cause us not to be thankful for them. (Deuteronomy 28:47,48) The one thing can cause us not to enjoy them. (2 Kings 7:1-3)

Beloved, I wish above all things that thou mayest prosper and be in health, even as thy soul prospereth. (3 John 2) There's just one thing.

You Are (UR) -- coming in loud and clear.

MAY 5 *(ACTS 10:1-4)*

Prayer is an interesting business with a protocol all its own. From preparation to salutation to content to intent, my bottom line is: Did God hear me and what's happening? Perhaps you remember the CB radio craze of yesteryear. *"Breaker, Breaker, 19. This here's your 'Holy Roller'. What's your 20? Come back."* You had to have the equipment. You had to know the lingo. And you had to be willing to develop relationships with people you trusted were out there.

Well, Jesus equipped and authorized you. (John 15:16) You can raise the Father, in Jesus' name, on the Holy Ghost band at any time. *"And this is the confidence we have in him, that if we ask any thing according to his will, he heareth us: and if we know that he hear us, whatsoever we ask, we know that we have the petitions that we desired of him."* (1 John 5:14) Call Him. He'll answer. Immediately. (Psalm 50:15/Jeremiah 33:3/ Daniel 10:1-12/Mark 11:23,24) He's got his ears on and help is on the way. And that's a big 10:4 (Acts 10:4 that is) good buddy.

You Are (UR) -- full of it.

MAY 6 *(ACTS 2:1-4)*

Say it out loud! I am filled with the Spirit of the living God. The same Holy Spirit that raised Jesus from the dead. The same Spirit that moved across the face of the waters just before God said; *"let there be light."* (Genesis 1:1-3) I am filled with the same Spirit that came upon and overshadowed Mary just before she said, *"Be it unto me according to thy word,"* and Jesus was impregnated in her womb. (Luke 1:34-48) That same Spirit dwells in me and quickens *(makes alive)* my mortal body. I am full to overflowing. My cup runs over. I am bubbling with rivers of living water that I don't even want to contain. (John 8:37,38) I am full of the Spirit of God.

You Are (UR) -- not going to believe it.

(ISAIAH 14:9-17) MAY 7

When you finally get a look at the devil, you are not going to believe your eyes. Forget "The Exorcist." Hollywood is just selling tickets. That's not him on the Deviled Ham can either. We are talking about Satan, Lucifer, Beelzebub, that old serpent called the Devil. You know, the one that was cast out of Heaven with all of his henchmen. The one that fell to the earth having great wrath, because he knows that his time is short. (Revelation 12:9-12)

I'm talking about the murderer, the liar, who when he speaks a lie he speaks his own, because he is a liar and the father of all lies. (John 8:44) This is your adversary, who walks about as a roaring lion seeking whom he may devour. (1 Peter 5:8) The one who doesn't even show up unless it is to steal, kill, and destroy (John 10:10), and when he does show up, it is as an angel of light. (2 Corinthians 11:14) But you are not ignorant of his devices.

You know God has given you power to tread on serpents and scorpions and all the power of the enemy. (Luke 10:19) Jesus defeated him on your behalf on the cross over two thousand years ago. Now you over-come him by the blood of the lamb and the word of your testimony. You cast out devils! (Mark 16:15-20) You submit yourself to God and the devil flees -- just as he did from Jesus. (James 4:7)

You are more than a conqueror because greater is he that is in you than he that is in the world. (1 John 4:4) You used to walk according to the course of this world, according to the prince of the power of the air. But God, who is rich in mercy, for his great love wherewith he loved us, even when we were dead in sins, has made us alive together with Christ (by grace we are saved). (Ephesians 2:1-5)

All of the above notwithstanding, when you see how powerless the devil really is and how weak and beggarly the elements of this world really are, (Galatians 4:9) you are probably not going to believe it.

You Are (UR) -- holy.

MAY 8 *(1 PETER 1:13-16)*

Say it out loud! Don't think about it. Don't balance your books. **Just say it!** I am holy as He is holy. I am a chosen generation, a royal priesthood. I am part of a holy nation. I am a peculiar person that should shew forth the praises of Him who hath called me out of darkness into His marvelous light. (1 Peter 2:9) People may question my holiness and call me *"holier than thou."* But how hard is it to be holier than someone who doesn't know Jesus? And why should I be ashamed to own up to such a high and holy calling?

I refuse to apologize, any longer, for that which God has made me, called me to, will judge me by, and has made available to all who will receive Him. Yes, I am holy. I am holy as He is holy. I am filled with the Holy Ghost. I am led by the Holy Spirit. I lift up holy hands to a holy God. And I cry holy, holy, holy, to Him that was and is and is to come. I used to be alienated and an enemy in my own mind, but now He has reconciled me in the body of His flesh through death, to present me holy and umblameable and unreproveable in His sight. I will continue in the faith grounded and settled, and be not moved away form the hope of the gospel. (Colossians 1:21-23) I am holy as He is holy.

You Are (UR) -- baptized into one body.

MAY 9 *(1 CORINTHIANS 12:12-31)*

You are a much needed member of the body. Your gifts, talents, skills, and abilities are y-o-unique and critical. So why aspire to be an eye when seeing is not your calling? The body has great need of you. God has set you in the body and His omniscience proves each day that what we once considered feeble is much more needful. There will be no you-ectomies here. You are a much needed member of the body.

You Are (UR) -- approved.

(2 Corinthians 10:18) We go through life looking for signs of approval. A pat on the back. An "A" on our report card. An application accepted. A life validated. But now we have the ultimate seal of approval. You have the Master's stamp - the mark that makes the difference. Paul understood it and made it clear when teaching the disciples about the pecking order of the world.

"Beware of dogs, beware of evil workers, beware of the concision. For we are the circumcision, which worship God in the spirit, and rejoice in Christ Jesus, and have no confidence in the flesh." (Philippians 3:1-14)

You are the circumcision. You have the mark in your heart that makes you acceptable unto God. You can get into the Holy of Holies. Sure, you've got your earthly validators -- natural acquisitions, accoutrements and accomplishments that you could brandish in a canine contest. But before you take aim on the nearest tree, remember: *"The kingdom of God is not meat and drink; but righteousness, and peace, and joy in the Holy Ghost."* Serve God in these and you are acceptable to God and approved of men. (Romans 14;17,18)

You Are (UR) -- in hot pursuit.

Our democratic documents state that we are endowed by God with certain inalienable rights: life, liberty and the pursuit of happiness. But this continual sense of endless *(for some hopeless and pointless)* pursuit can sometimes feel like a mixed blessing. It's you you're after, you know? As the "prodigal" son *"came to himself,"* so likewise, you are trying to catch what Jesus caught you for. **Hint:** {See 2/6} You are not that far away. (Romans 10:8-10)

You Are (UR) -- being watched.

MAY 12 *(2 CHRONICLES 16:9)*

Say it out loud! God has His eyes on me. Eyes, too pure to look on sin, are running to and fro throughout the whole earth as God shows Himself strong on my behalf. (Habakkuk 1:13) He is watching and He's got others watching too. Angels that I can't even see are watching out for me. (Hebrews 1:14/2 Kings 6) They have more than a panoramic view. They see into my past, present, and future. God and those that assist Him see my end from the beginning. And their outlook is positive. (Jeremiah 29:11) I am compassed about by a great cloud of witnesses. (Hebrews 12:1)

There is only one place I really need to look. I need to look to Jesus. My focus need not shift. I don't need to look to the right hand or the left. There is no need to look behind me. I know Goodness and Mercy are following me all the days of my life. (Psalm 23) I can look to the hills from whence cometh my help. My help comes from the Lord, which made heaven and earth. (Psalm 121) I can even close my eyes at night and rest, because he neither slumbers nor sleeps. As much as I don't always like what He sees, I like the fact that I am being watched and that it is God, Himself, that watches over me.

You Are (UR) -- standing on holy ground.

MAY 13 *(EXODUS 3:1-5)*

Don't look for any burning bushes. This note will have to serve as the oracle of the day. And unlike Moses, your boundaries are not limited to a little patch of mountainous ground. You are more like Joshua, in that *"every place that the sole of your foot shall tread upon, that has God given unto you."* (Joshua 1:3) In fact, there are no boundaries. All things are yours. (1 Corinthians 3:16-25) You are standing on holy ground.

You Are (UR) -- a winner.

(1 CORINTHIANS 15:57) MAY 14

"It doesn't matter if you win or lose. It's how you play the game."

Say it out loud! LIAR! LIAR! Pants on fire! People have taught adages like these, for years. Their goal being to promote good sportsmanship. Instead, they have created *"good losers."*

It does matter if you win or lose. And how you play the game often determines which you'll do. (1 Corinthians 9:19-27)

You Are (UR) -- a winner.

(HEBREWS 5:14-6:2) MAY 15

Winners master their fundamentals. I hated to play scales as a child. Like all youngsters, I wanted to play songs. But my dad insisted, *"there can be no creativity without discipline."* I soon learned the frustration of hearing music in my head that my fingers would not play. So many people imagine things that they will never *"real-eyes"* because they have not mastered their fundamentals. What lies between them and the thing they want to do are the things they refuse to do.

Fundamentals reveal limitations. When you work on them you find your strengths and weaknesses. You realize that you need to work on your dribble or your crossover. You find that you lost strokes inside the hundred yard marker or around the green. You become aware of *"the sin that so easily besets you."* (Hebrews 12:1,2) Now you know what to work on. Now you know how to plan your attack. You also know what to attack in your enemy, because he has weaknesses too. Yes, there are miracle shots and recoveries, but people who win consistently over a long period of time are not so spectacular. Because winners master their fundamentals.

You Are (UR) -- a winner.

MAY 16 *(JOHN 21:20-23)*

Winners understand the object of the game. You'd be surprised at how many people participate in activities without understanding or even caring about the object. They are there for the uniform or the trips or the adulation or the friendships. But watching them makes you wonder if they know what winning is.

End Zone dances and glass breaking slams. Driver from every tee box and newsmaking scams. They play the game like the losers they are. But winners keep their eyes on the prize. (Judges 7:4-7 / Philippians 3:13,14)

You Are (UR) -- a winner.

MAY 17 *(1 CORINTHIANS 9:25)*

Winners know and use the rules. I say *use* as opposed to *play by*, because the rules are more than a set of restrictions. Winners know that the rules can also be a point of advantage. Like a traffic signal, the rules can say go as well as slow down or stop. Many a champion has prevailed in what appeared to be dismal circumstances, because she knew and took advantage of the rules.

Michael Jordan's inbound pass off an opponent's back. Tiger Woods and friends moving a rock in a major. David's repentance after committing adultery and murder. (Psalm 51) Jehoshaphat's plea for God's promised deliverance when under attack. (2 Chronicles 20:5-9) These were all champions who knew and embraced the rules.

"Courage conquers all things."

Ovid

You Are (UR) -- a winner.

(2 CORINTHIANS 3:1-6) MAY 18

Winners discover and appreciate the nuances of the game. Because they know the object, understand the rules, and have mastered the fundamentals, they are able to apply subtle distinctions -- variations on the standard under special circumstances. A finger roll as opposed to a standard lay-up in heavy opposition. A low, two iron stinger in lieu of a driver on a windy day. Healing by word, shadow, mud or handkerchief, rather than laying on of hands. These are the signature moves winners make.

Losers, however, tend to be bound to traditional methods, or toward the opposite extreme, they try to imitate popularized nuances having forgotten the object, misunderstood the rules, and/or failed to master the fundamentals of the game. Either way, losers usually make a mess.

The Pharisees, for example, knew the rules but not the object of the game, so they struggled with Jesus' mud in the eye healing on the sabbath. (John 9) The sons of Sceva, toward the opposite extreme, tried to imitate Paul's *"special miracles"* but had not yet mastered the fundamentals of being born again and were soundly defeated by the devil. (Acts 19:11-16) But you are a winner. You discover and appreciate the nuances of the game.

You Are (UR) -- a winner.

(MATTHEW 2:1,2) MAY 19

Winners watch the stars. To a man, history's great champions were great students of history. They cherished stats and trivia. They learned strengths and weaknesses. They looked to the greats before them for information and inspiration. The Halls of Fame of Football, Baseball, Basketball, Golf, or Faith (Hebrews 11) are filled with stars of the past and future, because winners watch the stars.

You Are (UR) -- promised protection.

MAY 20 *(ISAIAH 49:22-25)*

I got an e-mail from one of our partners one day about a missing child. Sad to say, the abduction of children is becoming more and more common in our world. (2 Timothy 3:1-9) I spend a seemingly inordinate amount of time teaching my own daughter about the dangers of 'bad' people, while insisting that she expect and look for the good in all. That said, there is but so much we can do -- even in our prayers. (Romans 8:26) And that is the good news.

Thank God we have help beyond our human frailties. Imagine surrounding your children by a thousand of the world's finest bodyguards twenty-four hours a day, every day of their lives. Now imagine that these bodyguards are -- not of this world. (Psalm 91:10-12) That's God's promise to us and it's time we took Him up on it. You are promised protection.

You Are (UR) -- getting through.

MAY 21 *(DANIEL 10:10-12)*

Your prayers are making an impact. They are being heard and there *is* a response. You have God's promise that He will hear and answer when you call. (Mark 11:23,24) He will deliver you and you will glorify Him. (Psalm 50:15) God is not a man that He should lie. He said it. He will do it. (Numbers 23:19) Every prayer, every offering, every deed done to help those in need, is come up before Him for a memorial.

Now don't you forget His benefits. Your prayers are making an impact. Please don't let your conversation take it back. (Proverbs 14:23) You are getting through.

You Are (UR) -- my wife.
{To be read to your wife, or received from Jesus -- The Bridegroom}

(PROVERBS 18:22) MAY 22

I am so glad I found you. You are my good thing and I know that I am highly favored of the Lord. You are my help - - far more suitable (meet) than you will ever know. (Genesis 2:18) Thanks for aiding, undergirding, strengthening, and assisting me as I endeavor to fulfill the will of God in my life. I love you as I love myself. I cherish you and want only the best for you. (Ephesians 5:25-29) You are bone of my bone and flesh of my flesh. We are one in Him. You are my wife and I love you. *(Wives see 6/11)*

You Are (UR) -- not alone.

(GENESIS 2:18) MAY 23

God made the decision long ago: *"It is not good that the man should be alone."* From that day forward there has been family. There has also been opportunity for division, schism, strife, and the temptation to feel isolated and -- lonely. But you are not alone. You are connected by blood, water, and spirit to a family that fills heaven and earth. (Ephesians 3:14,15/Acts 17:24-48) You are connected by a common father, a common faith, and a common enemy. (Romans 4:13-25/1 Peter 5:8,9) Your adversary - the devil - would like to convince you that you are the only one in your situation. He would also love for you to continue in the belief that no one knows or cares how you feel or what you are going through. Most of all, he wants you to feel uniquely foolish in your failure. *"Nobody is as hopeless as you."*

But the devil is a liar. (John 8:44) He wants to isolate you from the faith and the family. (1 Timothy 4:1-2) The truth is -- what you are going through is quite common. (1 Corinthians 10:13) It is not new or unique. You are more than able to bear it. It didn't catch God by surprise. (Jonah 1:17/1 Corinthians 2:9,10) And there is a way out. People you haven't even met yet are praying for you and expecting your success. (Acts 12:1-19) So shake off your chains and run on home. You are not alone.

You Are (UR) -- not ashamed.

MAY 24 *(ROMANS 1:15-17)*

A muslim leader challenged me once, while I was preaching the gospel on the campus of UNC-CH. He called me intolerant and asked me to accept the fact that his beliefs were valid and just as capable of giving him audience with the *"One God"* as mine. I was unwilling to do any such thing and quoted him a barrage of scripture beginning and ending with John 14:6. He was livid - not to mention over six feet tall and almost three hundred pounds.

"Why must you always quote the Bible?" he bellowed. *(We had had this discussion before.)* "Why can't you speak to me using rhetoric and logic rather than dogma?" From a place purer and more powerful than my intellect, I responded, *"Why would I use a toothpick when I have sword?"* Why indeed? He retreated. And so will anyone else who challenges the unashamed. Why should you be ashamed? You are yelling **'FIRE!'** in a burning building. (Ezekiel 33:1-9) You know the only way to the candy store. (John 14:6) You have the cure for cancer. (Psalm 107:17-22 esp. v. 20) You have the words to eternal life. (John 6:66,67) You are not ashamed.

You Are (UR) -- a lively stone.

MAY 25 *(1 PETER 2:4,5)*

Say it out loud! I am a lively stone. I am built up a spiritual house. I am an holy priesthood and I offer up spiritual sacrifices. I present my body, a living sacrifice, holy, acceptable unto God by Jesus Christ. (Romans 12:1,2) I am no longer a child. I won't be tossed to and fro and carried about with every wind of doctrine. I will speak the truth in love and grow up into Jesus, my head, in all things. I am a lively stone, fitly joined together by that which every joint supplies. And the effective working of my part along with every other part makes increase of the body of Christ unto the building up of itself in love. (Ephesians 4:8-16)

You Are (UR) -- a breath of fresh air.

One of the strongest senses is the sense of smell. As we get closer to Memorial Day and the official start of summer, certain smells are going to become more and more common. A good whiff of mesquite or hickory on a backyard grill can take you through time and space to another era. Camp - camping - campus: It's more than food. It is fun, family, friends and fellowship. It's the smell of celery in boiling oil at the community fish fry behind Mr. Kelsey's house just before the Livingstone College Blue Bears' first home football game. Coach Marshall is devouring fish like Felix the Cat. Otis Redding is sitting on the dock of the bay. Daddy is dancing with momma. It's hot Sauce, hush puppies, and Coca-Cola. Everybody's happy, if just for today. God breathes deep and savors your impact on the world. This is the day that He has made. He remembers that Jesus didn't die in vain. You are a breath of fresh air.

You Are (UR) -- saying something.

I know you are because you walk by faith. You believed unto righteousness and confessed Jesus as Lord. (Romans 10:8-10) Now are you saved by grace through faith. (Ephesians 2:8-10) It was your faith that got you to righteousness, but now you have obtained "like precious" faith. (2 Peter 1:1-4) You have the substance of things hoped for -- the evidence of things not seen. (Hebrews 11:1) You must be saying something. Who wouldn't, if they knew they could have whatever they say? (Mark 11:22,23) With a heart and mouth full of world framing words on fire in you (Psalm 39/Matthew 12:34/2 Corinthians 4:13/James 4:1-12), being quiet must be the challenge. Or maybe it's knowing just what to say. After all, what you say is what you get -- calling things which be not as though they were just like God your father. (Romans 4:17) Hmmph. I know you are saying something.

You Are (UR) -- not a quitter.

MAY 28 *(HEBREWS 10:38,39)*

Say it out loud! I am not a quitter. I don't give up. I won't give up. I will continue in the faith. (Colossians 1:21-29) God is the author and the finisher of my faith. It is He that works in me both to will and to do of His good pleasure. (Philippians 2:12,13) I am confident of this very thing, that He which has begun a good work in me shall perform it until the day of Jesus Christ. (Philippians 1:6)

Normally, I would get tired. But Christ lives in me. And I know that the everlasting God, the Lord, the Creator of the ends of the earth faints not, neither is weary. He gives me power when I grow faint and increases my strength when it seems that I have no might. When I wait on Him, He renews my strength. I mount up with wings as eagles. I run and don't grow weary. I walk and don't faint. (Isaiah 4:28-31)

The joy of the Lord is my strength. (Nehemiah 8:8-10) I can run the race that is set before me with patience, looking unto Jesus, who for the joy that was set before Him, endured the cross, despising the shame, and is set down at the right hand of the throne of God. (Hebrews 12:1,2) And I am seated with Him in heavenly places. (Ephesians 2:6) The hard part is over. (Proverbs 13;15) I am not about to quit now. I am not a quitter.

You Are (UR) -- mine. (Jesus)

MAY 29 *(1 CORINTHIANS 3:18-21)*

Say it out loud! I belong to Christ. I didn't choose him. He chose me and ordained me that I should go and bring forth fruit and that my fruit should remain, so that whatever I ask of the father in Jesus' name he will give it to me. (John 15:16) I belong to Christ.

You Are (UR) -- Christ's.

You are Christ's. You belong to Him. You are His possession. And He is quite possessive -- Jealous even. (Exodus 34:14) I'm sure you have heard the saying: *"Possession is nine-tenths of the law."* Well, in His case, possession is all the law and the prophets. As a matter of fact, possession is all things. This journey we are on has a lot to do with possession.

Adam sold us into sin, giving the devil temporary ownership of our lives. Satan abused us so badly, for so long, that many of us forgot what we were, who we were, or whose we were. But Christ has redeemed us. He has bought us back with His blood. (Revelation 5:9) Now we are His. And if we be Christ's, then are we Abraham's seed and heirs according to the promise. (Galatians 3:26-28) All things are ours and we are Christ's and Christ is God's.

You Are (UR) -- the temple of God.

Outer Court, Inner Court, Holy of Holies. Body, Soul and Spirit, sanctified wholly. (1 Thessalonians 5:23) Stone upon living stone. Fitly framed together. (1 Peter 2:1-5) You are the temple of God. The holy flame of God's most Holy Spirit searches the inward parts of the belly and sends up a sweet savor to the most high. You are the temple -- the temple of God, where sacrifice is made and sins are forgiven.

You are God's holy habitation. (Ephesians 2:19-22) Ah, what a mystery that He would dwell in me. We who had no access to the temple made with hands. But now, the mystery is made manifest in the saints. God makes known what is the riches of the glory of this mystery among the Gentiles, which is Christ in you, the hope of glory. (Colossians 1:21-29) You are the temple of God.

You Are (UR) -- challenged to choose.

JUNE 1 *(JOSHUA 24:1-15)*

In a world filled with choices, we hate to choose. Give me a Russian Dozen. You know -- Onovich *(one of each)*. We are multi-tasking, "Jacks of All Trades," juggling multiple responsibilities, who want it all. And as Oprah says, *"You can have it all -- just not at the same time."* You have to choose. If thine eye be single, thy whole body shall be full of light. But if thine eye be evil (**Note:** There is no double or multiple. It's single or evil.) thy whole body shall be full of darkness. You can't serve two masters. (Matthew 6:22-24) A double minded man is unstable in all his ways. Let not that man *think* that he shall receive anything from the Lord. (James 1:5-8) In many cases, it's not even a matter of right or wrong. It's simply a matter of which one. Every minute brings millions more choices, but you are challenged to choose.

You Are (UR) -- charged with a choice.

JUNE 2 *(DEUTERONOMY 30:19,20)*

God sees the world filling up with choices around us, so he charges us with a choice. Life, death, blessing, cursing. **"CHOOSE LIFE!"** Some would argue: "That's no choice. If I get to choose, let me choose what I want to choose. Don't tell me what to choose." Okay. Choose. But make an informed choice. You do want to live don't you? You do want it to be well with you and yours don't you? Choose -- you may. Choose -- you must. You are challenged to choose. (Joshua 24:1-15) But you are also charged with a choice by one who can see the end and the outcome of all your options. Choose life, that both thou and thy seed may live.

You Are (UR) -- drawing closer to your goal.

(GENESIS 32:24-30) JUNE 3

Can you see the Lord?

Most of our strivings come from a place not so holy. James says, *"come they not hence, even of your lusts that war in your members?"* Self-preservation is a powerful force. *(The first law of nature, according to most.)* But which nature? Are we not partakers of the divine nature? Have we not escaped the corruption that is in the world through lust? (2 Peter 1:1-4)

Jacob deceived his brother Esau out of his birthright and had to flee to a life of labor for Laban, his deceitful father in-law. After years of lies and changed wages he made the decision to leave with his family and be reconciled to his brother. Terrified that Esau's wrath yet remained, he prayed for mercy from the most high God. It is in response to this prayer that we find him -- wrestling with the Lord. (Genesis 32:9-27)

When the sins of man forced God's hand to pour out the deluge in the days of Noah, God declared: *"My spirit shall not always strive with man."* Since that day, we have been grappling with everything and everyone in and around us. But Jesus has come to grant us the Spirit of repentance that we might return to God and each other.

There is yet one battle left to be won. One goal to pursue. One enemy to conquer. We must overcome the wicked one within us -- striving with the Spirit, as it were. (1 John 2:12-14) We must labour to enter into His rest. (Hebrews 4:1-11) Then and only then, can we return to the father and each other. You are drawing closer to your goal.

Can you see the Lord?

You Are (UR) -- in need of a cause.

JUNE 4 *(1 SAMUEL 17:17-29)*

Most people live their lives in response to B. Causes. *(Because I dropped out of high school. Because I got pregnant out of wedlock. Because I went to jail.)* You get the picture. We all have our B. Causes. They are external motivators that push us here and there like lifeless victims. They are the things you feel you have to do. *"I've got to keep this job." "I've got have this thing." "I've got to endure this abuse."*

Paul the Apostle overcame his great B. Cause (*"Because I persecuted the church of God"* 1 Corinthians 15:8-10) when Jesus revealed his A. Cause. An A. Cause is what you *must* do. (Acts 9:1-6) Now all of us won't get a revelation like Paul did. But A. Causes can come by revelation or by relationship. Jonathan's armorbearer overcame the B. Cause of an over-whelming number of enemy soldiers by aligning himself with Jonathan's A. Cause through relationship. *"Do all that is in thine heart,"* he said. *"Turn thee, behold, I am with thee according to thine heart."* Is your life on hold due to B. Causes? You are in need of a cause.

You Are (UR) -- selected and highlighted.

JUNE 5 *(2 TIMOTHY 4:1-4)*

In most word processing programs, the way to make changes to docu-ments is to select the area you wish to change and highlight it. Then you can correct things like spelling and grammar, or you can add or delete words. You can also make improvements like justification or making words bold. Jesus does the same thing by his word. He reproves, rebukes and exhorts. To reprove is to select and highlight. He shines the light of the word on us in particular. To rebuke is to make needed corrections. But to exhort is to warn and encourage. He has already justified us by his blood and his Spirit makes us bold. Jesus is the ultimate word processor.

You Are (UR) -- proof positive.

(ROMANS 12:1,2) JUNE 6

To those who doubt that God exists -- you are proof positive. (Hebrews 11:6) You prove that God forgives sin each time you forgive others. (Mark 11:22-25) You prove that He heals the sick when you walk in health and lay hands on others, expecting recovery. (3 John 2 / Mark 16:15-20) You prove that God meets needs when you give to those in need without so much as a second thought about your own. (Ephesians 4:17-32 esp. vs. 28) You prove that He protects us from all harm as you walk through life without fear, wrath, and doubting. (1 Timothy 2:1-8 / 2 Timothy 1:1-11) When you present your body a living sacrifice, holy, acceptable to God, *(the least any of us can do)* and refuse to act like the heathen of this world, but daily metamorphose into the nature of the most high by the continual renewing of your mind -- you are proof positive that the will of God is good, acceptable, and perfect.

You Are (UR) -- someone's joy and crown.

(PHILIPPIANS 4:1) JUNE 7

Someone, somewhere, rejoices in your salvation. Someone, somewhere, takes pleasure in your new life. All of heaven rejoiced when you, who were lost, were found. (Luke 15:1-7) And one day, someone, somewhere, will receive a crown of righteousness from the righteous judge, which is laid up for them along with all who love His appearing. (2 Timothy 4:7,8) Someone, somewhere, rejoices because you love His appearing.

His daily manifestations meet immediate needs. And it is good -- needful -- to believe to see His goodness, in the land of the living, lest we faint. (Psalm 27:13,14) But our rejoicing is not in the subjection of spirits unto us. We rejoice because our names are written in heaven. (Luke 10:17-20) Your name is written in heaven. You are someone's joy and crown.

You Are (UR) -- precious.

JUNE 8 *(PSALM 116:12-16)*

Don't mis-define precious as cute and sweet. Costly and valuable is what you are -- like silver or gold. You are an ambassador in the earth. (2 Corinthians 5:17-21) You are God's voice and hand to a dying generation. You have received Him and to you, He has given power to become a son of God. (John 1:12) You know the word and possess this world's good. (1 John 3:16-18) And God would like to keep you active and effective in the earth as long as possible.

Consider the fact that it costs a corporation thousands of dollars to train a new employee. Additionally, it is five times as hard to get a new customer as it is to keep an old one. Yes, heaven is wonderful and Jesus is preparing a place for you. (John 14:1-6) And believe it or not, the devil would love for you to go there. Heaven or hell, it doesn't matter to him. He knows that as long as you are on the earth, you do damage to his kingdom. Jesus is coming to get you. When He returns, let Him find you doing the will of God. Until then, remember: You are precious.

You Are (UR) -- seeing 'em like you call 'em.

JUNE 9 *(MARK 11:22,23)*

I know that's not how you learned the idiom *"Calling 'em like you see 'em."* But that explains the idiocy of most expectations and many situations. The scriptures are clear: What you say is what you get. If you keep talking about the way things are, they are destined to remain the same. Your heartfelt words have power. You possess the power of God to create with your tongue. (Proverbs 18:20,21) So if you want things to change, you had better trash your See & Say and get yourself a Say & See. Call those things that be not as though they were. (Romans 4:17) Believe that what God has said is true and agree -- *prophesy* -- with Him. (1 Samuel 10:1-6) Recreate your world through faith by the word of God, making things seen which do not appear. (Hebrews 11:3) Don't call 'em like you see 'em. Call 'em like He sees 'em and you'll see 'em like you call 'em.

You Are (UR) -- safe.

Say it out loud! I am safe. It's not that nothing is after me. The devil would like nothing more than to destroy me. He is walking about as a roaring lion, looking for someone just like me to devour. (1 Peter 5:8) It's not personal. He's a good devil. He's just doing his job. He hates God and he knows that God loves me. He can't beat God so he comes after me. But the good news is: He can't beat me either.

Greater is He that is in me than he that is in the world. (1 John 4:4) No weapon that is formed against me shall prosper. (Isaiah 54:17) I have been given power to tread on serpents and scorpions and over all the power of the enemy. (Luke 10:17-20) I don't have to do wicked things as I flee from people and things that neither pursue nor would prevail if they did. (Proverbs 28:1) I'm safe. I don't have to run from the devil or anyone else. I don't have to lash out or fight back or put up my dukes. I'm safe. Safe and secure from all alarm. I am dwelling in the secret place of the most high. (Psalm 91) My life is hid with Christ in God. (Colossians 3:1-3) Even in death -- I'm safe. (2 Corinthians 5:1-7)

You Are (UR) -- my husband.
{To be read to your husband and/or to Jesus -- The Bridegroom}

I am so glad you sought me out. You are my head and the saviour of our body. I submit myself to you, without fear, in everything. I will obey you that you may cover me with joy. I know this is profitable for me. You are my lord/Lord. You are my love. We are one.

I am bone of your bone and flesh of your flesh and we will walk compassionately with one another. I will love you as my brother. Pitifully and courteously, I will dwell with you in unity and be a crown unto your head. I love you. I reverence you. You are my husband. *(Husbands see 5/22)*

You Are (UR) -- not seeing things.

JUNE 12 *(ACTS 12:1-9)*

Sometimes the power of God's deliverance can seem too good to be true. All the circumstances point to certain destruction. We're surrounded. They've got us. And, in many cases, we believe we deserve it. Some of us have actually given up and asked God to just take us or let us die. (1 Kings 19:1-4) But what we forget is that we are not the only ones praying. (1 Kings 19:14-18)

Around the world, unheralded saints are faithful. They pray without ceasing. (1 Thessalonians 5:17) They pray for all men everywhere -- including you. (1 Timothy 2:1-4) They pray with groanings that cannot be uttered, overriding their natural understanding. They pray according to the will of God. (Romans 8:26-28 / 1 Corinthians 14:14,15) They pray in faith believing and God answers. (Mark 11:22,23) For even when we are unfaithful, He remains faithful. And though we deny Him, He cannot deny Himself. (2 Timothy 2:11-13)

We are the blessed beneficiaries of faith beyond our own. Angels show up and deliver us. It can sometimes seem too good to be true. But don't let flesh and natural expectation cause you to miss a blessing. You are not seeing things. The prison doors are open. You are free. God's expectation has once again superseded the expectation of the enemy. (Jeremiah 29:11) And you have the victory. (1 Corinthians 15:57)

So run. Run to where the saints are gathered. Run to sing God's praises and offer up thanksgiving. You may find that they think they're seeing things, too. That's okay. You are still free.

"He who is not courageous enough to take risks
will accomplish nothing in life."

Muhammad Ali

You Are (UR) -- not hearing things.

Young Samuel heard the voice of the Lord and did not know who it was. He ran to Eli, the priest, his legal guardian, because his mother had given him to the temple when he was weaned. *"Here am I,"* he said. Three times this happened before Eli told him it was the Lord.

I heard that very voice more than twenty years ago. *"You are twenty-two years old. You have a good education. You have good friends. You are very gifted. But you will ruin it all if you continue to live like you're living."* It was unmistakable. And though, like Samuel, I had no idea who it was, I understood the message. I quit doing drugs that day. I had my last beer a few weeks later. And I gave my life to Jesus within ninety days of that warning.

God still speaks. Through His word. Through His servants. Through that still, small voice inside. Some people call it intuition -- being taught from within. Others call it conscience. Co-science. The cooperation between two kinds of knowledge. *(What you know of you. What you know of God. And how they relate to each other.)*

Call it what you want, but you are not hearing things. *"For to him that knoweth to do good and he doeth it not it is sin."* (James 4:17) And *"happy is he that condemns not himself in that thing which he allows."* (Romans 14:19-23) *"For the invisible* (inaudible) *things of him from the creation of the world are clearly seen* (and heard)*, being understood by the things that are made, even his eternal power and God-head, so that they are without excuse."* (Romans 1:20)

You are not hearing things.

"Courage is grace under pressure."

Ernest Hemingway

You Are (UR) -- flying a new flag.

JUNE 14 *(EXODUS 17:8-16)*

After Israel's glorious victory over the Amelekites, *"Moses built an altar and called the name of it Jehovah Nissi."* Loosely translated, that is the Lord our banner or flag.

It is a common practice of war that when a victory is won and an enemy conquered, the victor captures the enemy's flag and raises his own. So it is with us. The devil is defeated. His reign of terror has been overthrown and God's banner of love now flies over our lives. He has led captivity captive and given gifts unto men. (Ephesians 4:8) Truly, we *"are a chosen generation, a royal priesthood, an holy nation."* (1 Peter 2:9)

On this flag day, His banner of love waves gloriously over us. We are proudly flying a brand new flag.

You Are (UR) -- wise.

JUNE 15 *(PROVERBS 11:30,31)*

You were born smart. Your mother said so early on. Who am I to argue with your mother? But if you're like me, you've done a few things, since then, to make even mom question her opinion. You have been well educated. Well -- you've been educated to some degree. But wisdom is measured in an entirely different way. Wisdom is an internal awakening that clarifies your surroundings. Wisdom increases the value of time while narrowing one's scope of purpose. In other words, you are wise when you wake up, see what's really going on around you, and get busy doing something specific about it. Mom's approval and the conferred degrees of institutions of higher learning notwithstanding, wisdom is validated by God and measured in souls. (Ephesians 5:14) You are wise -- aren't you?

You Are (UR) --renewed; day by day.

(2 Corinthians 4:13-16) JUNE 16

Feeling tired and run down? Perhaps you feel like a has-been or maybe even a never-was. Worn out or washed up? Burned so many times you're burned out. You don't need Geritol, Serutan, S-S-S Tonic, Club Med or a vacation. You need to stop confusing outward-man banality with inward-man reality.

Your body is at war with your spirit. (Galatians 5:16-18) You -- *soul man* -- are deciding who wins. (Genesis 2:7) You have been quickened by the same Spirit that raised Christ from the dead. (Romans 8:11) You are made alive by the same Spirit that moved across the waters when darkness covered the face of the deep, just before God said: *"Let there be light."* (Genesis 1:1-3) You are a son of God because you are led by the same Spirit that overshadowed Mary, empowering her as He came upon her and she said, *"Be it unto me according to your word."* (Romans 8:14 / Luke 1:34-38)

You are being transformed by the renewing of your mind. (Romans 12:1,2) And even the time you've lost or wasted is being restored. (Joel 2:25) See it in the word. Empower it by the Spirit. Say it from your heart. "I am renewed -- day by day."

You Are (UR) -- fearfully and wonderfully made.

(Psalm 139:13,14) JUNE 17

You are marvelous. If there is any doubt, take it from the one that made you and get it down in you so that you know it like you know your name. As my grandmama would say, *"God don't make no junk."*

Say it out loud! *"I will praise thee; for I am fearfully and wonderfully made: marvelous are thy works; and that my soul knoweth right well."*

You Are (UR) --well staffed.

JUNE 18 *(2 CORINTHIANS 4:17,18)*

"I could use some help." "I don't have any help." "Good help is so hard to find." I have heard and made these comments throughout my life -- usually in the face of trouble. Well, imagine my surprise, when I discovered that God had packaged the help in the problems. (Romans 8:26 / 1 Corinthians 10:13) We're surrounded by able workmen. What we need is a plan.

Imagine a hundred volunteers showing up at your door today. Would they help or hinder you? Don't answer too quickly. Is your vision written clearly enough so that you could divide yourself and make real progress? (Habakkuk 2:1-4 / Genesis 14:12-16) Or would you have to stop what you were doing to figure out what to do with them and eventually wind up getting rid of them or just giving them busy work while you suffered the headaches of having them around? Suddenly James 1 makes sense. If you've got problems -- you've got help. You are well staffed. What you need is a plan.

You Are (UR) -- in need of patience.

JUNE 19 *(HEBREWS 10:35-39)*

You have done the will of God. You have repented. You are saved. You will not perish because you have come to the knowledge of the truth. (1 Timothy 2:1-4 / 2 Peter 3:9) There are great and precious promises established for you that you might take your part of the divine nature. You have escaped the corruption that is in the world. (2 Peter 1:1-4) Don't quit. Don't give up. Don't faint. Don't grow weary in well doing. You shall reap. (Galatians 6:7-9) Your season is coming. It must, because the earth remains and God can't lie. (Genesis 8:22 / Titus 1:1-4) Now is not the time to murmur and complain. Now is the time to rejoice. You will be tried, tempted, tested, and tricked. Count it all joy. Patience is being worked in you and that is exactly what you need. Soon and very soon, you will be perfect and entire, wanting nothing. (James 1:1-5)

You Are (UR) -- what you are by the grace of God.

(1 CORINTHIANS 15:1-10) JUNE 20

"That's just the way I am." I've heard people say that for years. I have probably said it myself. Some even go so far as to say: *"That's just the way God made me."* Even Popeye the Sailor declared the limitations of his animated being. *"Iyam what Iyam and that's all Iyam."*

All jokes aside, such declarations should be translated: *"This is what I have become and I don't believe I can change."* That's why I like Paul the apostle's, declaration best. *"But by the grace of God I am what I am."*

Paul *(formerly Saul of Tarsus)* discovered who he really was on the road to Damascus. (Acts 9:1-16/Acts 26:1-20 esp. vs 19) He knew he had dodged a bullet. He knew he hadn't gotten where he was on his own. He knew he deserved to die and go to hell. He could even tell you why. (1 Cor. 15:9) But rather than define himself by what he knew, he chose to accept the definition of He who knew him best and become something far more gracious.

You Are (UR) -- loaded.

(PSALM 68:19) JUNE 21

When the queen of Sheba came to see King Solomon in 950 BC, she did not come empty-handed. She came to Jerusalem with a very great train, with camels that bore spices, and gold, and precious stones. (1 Kings 10:1-3) You don't go anywhere empty-handed either. Everywhere you go -- you go loaded. God daily loads you with benefits. Is it possible you have forgotten them? The queen unloaded her treasure on Solomon in response to the wisdom he shared. When we begin to unload our benefits on the world, they will respond as well. **Say it out loud!** I am loaded!

You Are (UR) -- incomparable.

JUNE 22 *(2 CORINTHIANS 10:12-18)*

If the world around you is not responding to you in the way that it should -- it may be that it doesn't recognize you. All things are yours. (1 Corinthians 3:18-21) And the things know it. They want to be in subjection so that they can be free from the foolishness of unrighteous ownership. They are simply waiting for the manifestation of the sons of God. (Romans 8:18,19)

But so many of us have been seduced. (Proverbs 12:26) We are measuring our success, victory, achievement, and even blessedness by world standards. Better than the world. More than the world. Best in the world. The only problem is -- there is none good in the world -- no not one. (Romans 3:9,10)

God's approval is our measure of success. (Acts 2:22) And the line differs for every man. I have a course to finish. (2 Timothy 4:7) You have a race to run. (Hebrews 12:1,2) We all have our own salvation to work out and that with fear and trembling. (Philippians 2:12,13)

The angels are prepared to minister on our behalf. (Hebrews 1:14) The devil is prepared to flee. (James 4:7) Trees and hills are ready to obey. But only in response to the real you. The voice, the vocation, and the visage have to match. There is no one else like you.

The hairs on your head are numbered. (Matthew 10:29-31) These are serial numbers that match your expected end like an identification card or user name and password that are required to access resources and claim rewards. A stolen or expired ID or incorrect user name or password will elicit cool, if not hostile, responses. So if the world around you is not responding to you in the way that it should -- it may be that it doesn't recognize you.

PS *Lost your ID or Forgotten your username or password? Contact the manufacturer at:* **PSA-5015** (That's Psalm 50:15)

You Are (UR) -- a workman.

Say it out loud! I am a workman. I don't have time to get caught in foolish arguments over silly semantics that do nothing but pull the rug from under the people who hear me. I need and want God's approval. And I certainly don't need or want to be embarrassed at the end of the day because I got it all wrong. So I am avoiding vulgar and unfruitful, mindless chatter because it will just contribute to the ungodliness that I am here to combat.

I've got work to do. I've got a world to win. I'm cleaning up my act so that God can use me. Later for the kid stuff. I am after the fruit of the Spirit. (Galatians 5:16-26) No more nit-picking and gawking at gnats. I am a gentle, able, willing teacher. I will persevere as long as it takes. I know that there are people out there who are destroying their own lives. And if God will give them the desire to change and come to the knowledge of the truth, I am ready to help them get away from the devil who is ruling their lives. I am a workman. I've got work to do.

You Are (UR) -- selling yourself cheap.

How many times have you agreed to work for a price, only to bemoan the deal you made on payday. Perhaps you discover that someone else is making more for the very same job. Or maybe you find that the budget would have allowed for more that you requested. In any case, remember - no one held a gun to your head.

You walked in the door with a sense of personal value and agreed to what you agreed to. Want more? Ask for more. (2 Samuel 12:7,8 / James 4:1,2) Sure, some people will laugh you out the door as they say "No!" But when "Yes" arrives, and it surely will, you will be doubly glad that you stopped selling yourself cheap.

You Are (UR) -- the voice of victory.

JUNE 25 *(EZEKIEL 37)*

The valley was full of dead men's bones, bleached white from time and exposure. Wanna, Gonna, and Mighta had long since left town with Shoulda, Woulda, and Coulda. But God asked a question: *"Son of man, can these bones live?"* And Ezekiel answered as most men do. *"O Lord God, thou knowest."*

Yes, He does. But do you? Do you know that He will never leave you nor forsake you? (Hebrews 13:5) Do you know that He shall supply all your need? (Philippians 4:19) Do you know that He wishes above all things that you may prosper and be in health even as your soul prospers? (3 John 2) Do you know that He is not willing that you should perish? (2 Peter 3:9) He knew He would deliver Israel. But Moses had the rod and commanded the sea to divide. He knew He would raise Lazarus. But Jesus said; "Come forth." He knew He would save you from your sins. But you said, *"I repent."* God has great expectations for you. But you are the voice of victory.

You Are (UR) -- a whoso(ever).

JUNE 26 *(JOHN 3:16)*

You are the reason God gave his only begotten son. You should not perish but have everlasting life. You have called upon the name of the Lord; you shall be saved. *(Saved from condemnation of sin. Saved from sickness and disease. Saved from poverty and lack. Saved from all of life's calamities.)* You offer praise and glorify God. You have ordered your conversation aright and you see the salvation of God. (Psalm 50:23) You have a willing heart. (Exodus 35:5 / Isaiah 1:19.20) You live and believe in Jesus -- you shall never die. (John 11:25,26) You shall not be ashamed. (Romans 9:33) You don't sin. (1 John 3:6-9) You are born of God. You love the father and you love the son. (1 John 5:1) You are a whoso(ever).

You Are (UR) -- going to the other side.

My daughter was taking swimming lessons. Float. Push off. Glide. Kick. Stroke. *"I can't breathe!"* It had all the makings for a traumatic experience. Not for her -- for me! Then came the big day. She had to swim from one side of the pool to the other. So the day before, some familiar spirits showed up. Fear. I can't. Quit. But that night we learned one extra lesson. Prophesy.

Say it out loud! I am going to the other side!

Jesus told the disciples, *"Let us pass over to the other side."* Then he went to sleep. The storm came up. Fear, I can't and Quit blew in. *"Lord don't you care that we're gonna die?"* But Jesus got up and prophesied. *"Peace! Be still."* Gabrielle went to the other side. Did she meet Fear, I can't and Quit on the way? Certainly. But ask her where she's going and she will tell you. I am going to the other side! {See July 1}

You Are (UR) -- called to be...

A fish will die doing fish-like things
A dog, like dogs, the same
Swim or bark, no matter where
By any other name
Called to be
Like you and me
I know why the caged bird sings
For called to be...obedience
Will do no other thing

Pssst: Don't know what to do? Obey the heavenly vision. (Acts 26:19)

You Are (UR) -- beautiful.

JUNE 29 *(ISAIAH 61:1-3)*

Wait! Before you drag your vanity to the mirror -- that was a gift. Wait! Before you gather the pieces of your vanity from the floor -- I mean the beauty was a gift. Isn't it strange, that with the exception of a few of our more vain/arrogant friends, most of us rely on the opinions of others to measure or validate our attractiveness. We have tried to protect our insecurities about comparative beauty standards with clichés like, Beauty is fleeting. Beauty's only skin deep. And Beauty is in the eye of the beholder. None of which are true. Beauty is eternal. Beauty is all encompassing. Because beauty is in the hand of the creator. And He says -- you are beautiful. (Ecclesiastes 3:11)

PS How beautiful? As beautiful as the gospel you preach. You bring glad tidings of good things. You are covered with the oil of joy and the garment of praise. And all who behold you -- yea, all who believe you -- are restored, set free and comforted. (Romans 10:13-15)

You Are (UR) -- looking quite becoming.

JUNE 30 *(EPHESIANS 6:10-20)*

It has been said that clothing makes the man. If that is so, then you, my friend, are a -- made man. You have put on the garment of praise for the spirit of heaviness. WOW! It looks good on you. Praise is definitely comely for the upright. And you must be upright. You are wearing the breastplate and the robe of righteousness. As a matter of fact, all of your garments are garments of salvation. From your head to your feet, you are looking a lot like Jesus. That helmet of salvation is saying something. Sharper than any Church of God In Christ Sunday best. Your loins are girt about with nothing but the truth. And those shoes. Let's just say that the preparation of the gospel of peace will always be the premier purveyor of beautifying footwear. Shield of faith and sword of the Spirit, you are accessorized perfectly. You are looking quite becoming. You are becoming more like Jesus.

You Are (UR) -- almost home.

(LUKE 15:20) JULY 1

Don't give up. Don't quit. Don't look back. You're almost home. The hard part is over. You made it through death and lived. (Galatians 2:20) Now you are helped by the comforter. He is helping your infirmities. (Romans 8:26) Lean in. Press for the tape. (Philippians 3:13,14) Give it all you've got. Father's waiting. You're almost home.

You Are (UR) -- loud, delirious and redundant.

(PSALM 35:27) JULY 2

Sounds like you're drunk. Don't be ashamed. That puts you in mighty good company. Eli thought Hannah was drunk. (1 Samuel:1-17) The multitude thought Peter and the 120 were plastered. (Acts 2:1-13) They told Bartimaeus to be quiet. (Mark 10:46-52) And the importuning widow just kept asking for the same thing until she wore the king down. (Luke 18:1-8)

While the world around us is quietly trying to stay off the radar screen, fearful of the next barrage of bad news and changing their conversation every other day to rehearse the latest mishap, we are like drunken men and women singing the same old song. We're drunk on new wine and we see something they don't see.

We are excited, hopeful and happy and our hearts are filled with illogical, unexplainable, praise-producing peace. Sure, they'll call you loud, delirious and annoyingly redundant. But you keep on shouting for joy and being glad. You keep on saying: *"Let the Lord be magnified, which hath pleasure in the prosperity of his servant."* Chances are, they'll call you when they need you.

You Are (UR) -- an insider.

JULY 3 *(EPHESIANS 2:1-12)*

Say it out loud! I am an insider. I used to be outside. Outside the commonwealth of Israel. Outside the covenants of promise. Without hope and without God in the world. I had no access. (Romans 5:1,2) The door of the "ark" was closed. (Genesis 7:11-16) But Jesus let me in by a new and living way. His broken body became my torn veil -- my at/one/ment -- my portal -- my way back. He became my new and living way in. (Hebrews 10:19,20) In is better than out. Up is better than down. Life is better than death. Blessing is better than cursing. Heaven is better than hell. And Jesus is better than anything and everyone. He kicked the devil out -- out of heaven -- out of the garden -- out of my life. And he invited me in -- into salvation -- into life -- into eternity. I am an insider!

You Are (UR) -- unentangled.

JULY 4 *(GALATIANS 5:1)*

As we celebrate America's independence, let us cherish our freedom. Freedom from condemnation of sin. Freedom from sickness and disease. (Isaiah 53:3-5) Freedom from poverty and lack. (Matthew 6:23-34) Freedom from all of life's calamities. (Isaiah 54:17) We are free indeed. (John 8:36) Christ has made us free. Freedom in America, is the freedom to be like everyone else. To have what they have. To do what they do. "All men are created equal." But they weren't created to stay that way. (Philippians 2:12,13) The cost of freedom in America is the continual pressure of everyone else to be like them. To have what they have. To do what they do. Alexis DeTocqueville called it "The tyranny of the majority." Paul called it conforming to this world. (Romans 12:1-8) The scriptures warn against the seduction of the wicked. You are more excellent than your neighbor. So now that you are free. Stay free!

You Are (UR) -- as a tree planted by the waters.

It's hot in this neck of the woods. Water is a valuable commodity. Fortunately, we have a lot of rain most years, but every now and then, we experience drought. Now it seems that the threat of drought is constant elsewhere. The economy. The markets. The jobs situation. Lay offs here. Plant closings there. You've heard the prognosticators and the prophets of doom. Many are fearful. But not you. Now let's remember why.

Say it out loud!
God has not given me the spirit of fear, but of power, and of love, and of a sound mind. (2 Timothy 1:7) I AM as a tree planted by the waters. My roots are spread out. I could say that I should not worry when trouble comes. But the scriptures say that I will not even see when trouble comes. Why? Because I look not at the things which are seen. I look at the things which are not seen. I walk by faith and not by sight. (2 Corinthians 5:7)

Through faith I understand that the worlds were framed by the word of God so that things which are seen were not made of things which do appear. (Hebrews 11:3) I know that the things which are seen are temporary. But the things which are not seen -- *the promises of God, the power of God, the angels of God, the Spirit of God* -- are eternal. (2 Corinthians 4:16-18)

Conditions will change. And circumstances will change. But I serve the everlasting God who changes not. (Malachi 3:6) I am as a tree planted by the rivers of water.

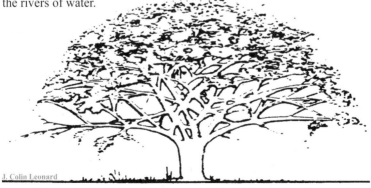

J. Colin Leonard

You Are (UR) -- a blessing.

JULY 6 *(GENESIS 12:1-3)*

Say it out loud! I belong to Christ. And if I belong to Christ then I am Abraham's seed and an heir according to the promise. (Galatians 3:26-29) God promised Abraham that he would make him a great nation and that he would bless him. God promised Abraham that he would make his name great and that he would be a blessing. God promised Abraham that he would bless them that bless Abraham and curse them that curse Abraham and that in Abraham all families of the earth would be blessed.

God is not a man that he should lie, neither the son of man that he should repent. If he said it, he will do it. If he spoke it, he will make it good. (Numbers 23:19) God didn't bless Abraham just so he could be blessed. He blessed Abraham to be a blessing. I belong to Christ! I am Abraham's seed and an heir according to the promise. I am blessed. I am a blessing!

You Are (UR) -- coming out.

JULY 7 *(1 PETER 2:9,10)*

Say it out loud! I am coming out! I am coming out of bondage. I am coming out of fear. I am coming out of sickness and disease. I am coming out of poverty, debt and lack. I am coming out of sin! I am coming out of any and everything that is not like God. The children of Israel did it and so can I. They came out because God brought them out. And the same God -- the God of Abraham, Isaac, Jacob and me -- is bringing me out too.

They came out with their little ones, their old and their young, and there was not a feeble one among them. They came out with full compensation for their labor in Egypt. They grew weary of their bondage. They cried to their God and He heard their voice. He looked on their affliction and He brought them out with an outstretched arm and a mighty hand and with great terribleness, and with signs and wonders. (Deuteronomoy 26:1-9) He has not changed and He is no respecter of persons. I am coming out!

You Are (UR) -- going through.

Everyone had quoted their favorite scripture at the church anniversary. (John 3:16 / The 23rd Psalm / 2 Corinthians 5:17 / Philippians 4:19) Ninety-seven year old Deacon Brown was last. He stood slowly and proudly and in his signature stentorian voice proclaimed, *"And it came to pass."* and calmly sat down. The pastor respectfully prodded, "Deacon Brown, there are many scriptures that begin *'And it came to pass...'* which one did you have in mind?" *"That's my favorite part, pastor."* Deacon Brown resolutely replied.

The pastor, knowing these waters ran much deeper, persisted. "Well Deac, there are a lot of young saints here who would love to know just what you get from those words; would you mind elaborating?" *"Pastor,"* the church's elder statesman said as he rose again, *"I'm ninety-seven years old and I've been through a lot on this journey with the Lord."* Everyone leaned in hoping to grasp the secret of Deacon Brown's success, both naturally and spiritually. *"The one thing I have learned is,"* he paused as though reflecting, *"when trouble came -- it never came to stay. It came to pass."*

You Are (UR) -- going to fall.

It was very natural, though unrehearsed. Reasonable, though unexpected. Falling was the only thing to do. The staggering combination of relaxing under the relentless stress of my troubles, the dizzying shift of focus from that which pursued me to He who would deliver me, and a sudden lunge through a newly revealed way of escape toward the source of my relief. It was my first encounter with worship. My brain said: *"You are going to fall."*

You Are (UR) -- coming in.

JULY 10 *(EPHESIANS 2:8-10)*

People dream of and talk about the day their ship will "come in." Sociologists call it the cargo cult mentality. It is the notion that one day a ship will arrive in the harbor with every wonderful thing that you have ever wished for. *(The lottery, an inheritance, supernatural debt reduction, the great wealth transfer, Mr. Right -- give it a name).* But suppose, for a moment, that you are that ship. Suppose, for a moment, that you have been sailing around aimlessly, like the "prodigal" son, needing to come to yourself.

God has brought you out of bondage. He has loosed you from the snares of the enemy. He is bringing you through manifold temptations. (1 Peter 1:3-9) And you are surrounded by storms and troubled waters. But while you gaze longingly off the bow, waiting for something good to come to you, you are neglecting the cargo that you carry. (1 Timothy 4:11-16) It is you that must proclaim, *"Peace! Be still."* (Mark 4:35-41) It is God that worketh in you both to will and to do of his good pleasure. (Philippians 2:12,13) It is you that will bring forth out of your treasure things old and new. (Matthew 13:52) He brought you out. He has carried you through. You are coming in.

You Are (UR) -- surrounded by miracles.
{Thank you to all who serve, naturally or spiritually.}

JULY 11 *(1 CORINTHIANS 12:1-11)*

Miracles, like fire trucks, are amazing, larger than life, problem solvers, that everyone should be able to call for and expect them to arrive. But the only people who should see them up close, every day, are the people who work them. These are people who have made the commitment to serve others, having prepared themselves to spend their lives, addressing the dangers and horrors that demand such solutions. Need a miracle? Call! (Romans 10:13) Want to see miracles every day? Make the commitment.

You Are (UR) -- behind that preposition.

(EPHESIANS 2:8-10) JULY 12

There are two notable throughways in Charleston, SC -- Coming Street and Meeting Street. There is, however, no Going Street. This may explain the city's population explosion and its ever increasing economic development. It is not uncommon for the natives to ask us 'comeyahs' (people who have come here from elsewhere) where we live at. My upbringing always forces me to think, if not say, "Behind that preposition."

God has strategically pre-positioned us. He knew where we would be before there was an *"at"* to be behind. He has brought us out of bondage into His glorious liberty. (Galatians 5:1) He has brought us out of darkness into His marvelous light. (1 Peter 2:9,10) And though we may go through manifold temptations, He expects the trial of our faith to be found unto praise and honour and glory at the appearing of Jesus Christ. (1 Peter 1:3-9) God foreordained (pre-positioned) our victory before the foundation of the world so that Coming, Meeting, or Going, we can always be found in Him. (Philippians 3:7-12)

You Are (UR) -- on God's mind.

(PSALM 8:1-4) JULY 13

Consider how forgetful you can be and then remember that God never forgets you. Everything you are concerned about is a concern for Him. (Psalm 138:8) He is aware of who you are, where you are, and most importantly, what you are. (Psalm 103:14) You are His workmanship, created in Christ Jesus unto good works which He has before ordained that you should walk in them. (Ephesians 2:8-10) He is ordering your steps and will pick you up if/when you fall. (Psalm 37:23,24) And if you ever wonder what He is thinking about, always know, you are on His mind.

You Are (UR) -- wiser than your enemies.

JULY 14 *(PSALM 119:97-104)*

Today, is Bastille Day. In honor of this celebration of freedom, I give you one of France's great statesmen on the subject of meditation.

> *"Men who live in democratic communities not only seldom indulge in meditation, but they naturally entertain very little esteem for it. A democratic state of society and democratic institutions keep the greater part of men in constant activity; and the habits of mind which are suited to an active life are not always suited to a contemplative one. The man of action is frequently obliged to content himself with the best he can get, because he would never accomplish his purpose if he chose to carry every detail to perfection. He has perpetually occasion to rely on ideas which he has not had leisure to search to the bottom; for he is much more frequently aided by the seasonableness of an idea than by its strict accuracy; and, in the long run, he risks less in making use of some false principles, than in spending his time in establishing all his principles on the basis of truth. The world is not led by long or learned demonstrations: a rapid glance at particular incidents, the daily study of the fleeting passions of the multitude, the accidents of the moment and the art of turning them to account, decide all its affairs."*

Alexis DeTocqueville -- Democracy In America

You Are (UR) -- resting.

JULY 15 *(HEBREWS 4:1-11)*

Sometimes taking a break is the hardest work we do. God knew this and it is why He established the sabbath. "The sabbath was made for man, and not man for the sabbath," (Mark 2:23-28) Jesus said. The sabbath was designed to prove to us that six days' work with trust in God can yield far more than continuous labor on its own. So when people ask what you are doing, tell them, without shame, *"I'm resting."*

You Are (UR) -- blessed indeed.

(1 CHRONICLES 4:9,10) JULY 16

Little Amy came home from school crying. *"What's wrong?"* her mother asked. *"No one at school will play with me. I don't have any friends."* Mom hugged her and gently reminded Amy that she had Jesus -- a friend that sticks closer than a brother. Later that night, mom heard Amy cry after she had tucked her in. *"What's the matter, sweetie?"* Mom inquired. Amy looked at mom with teary brown eyes and declared, *"I need friends with skin on them."*

Jabez, like Amy, dared to pray what so many of us think. *"Oh that thou wouldest bless me indeed."* In other words, *"I read it. I hear it. And I say it. But I don't see. And I'm tired of being paper rich and pocket poor. Lord -- bless me where I can feel it!"* David knew that feeling. He said: *"I had fainted unless I had believed to see the goodness of the Lord in the land of the living."* (Psalm 27:13) Ours is not merely a paper blessing. The Spirit brings life to the letter. Wait on the Lord as David did. Press in like the woman with the issue of blood. (Mark 5:25-34) Call on God like Jabez. If you don't, you'll grow resentful and frustrated like the "prodigal" son's older brother. (Luke 11:25-32) Remember: Hope deferred makes the heart sick. (Proverbs 13:12) Thank God! You are not just blessed in word. You are blessed indeed.

You Are (UR) -- converted.

(LUKE 22:31,32) JULY 17

Jesus told Peter that the devil was out to get him. He's out to get you, too. But Jesus assured Peter that He was praying for him. Jesus is praying for you, too. Jesus asked *(demanded)* only one thing of Peter. *"When thou art converted, strengthen thy brethren."* You are converted. You are changed. You are a new creature in Christ Jesus. (2 Corinthians 5:17) You have become another man. (1 Samuel 10:1-6) Strengthen the brethren.

You Are (UR) -- tongue-tied.

JULY 18 *(JAMES 3:1-13)*

Your life is led, bound, wrapped and shaped by the words of your mouth. 'Tongue-tied' is an expression that is generally used to describe an inability to speak or find the words to express ourselves. If only that were the case. Silence, in most cases would be golden. But our difficulty comes, more often than not, from what we express rather than what we suppress. David said, *"I will take heed to my ways, that I sin not with my tongue: I will keep my mouth with a bridle, while the wicked is before me."* (Psalm 39:1) As long as we are on this earth, the wicked will be before us, and David had it right. You are what you are. You have what you have. You do what you do. Your entire world is framed by the words of your mouth. (Hebrews 11:3) If you are not happy with what you see, check what you say. If you are stuck, for better or for worse -- you are tongue-tied.

You Are (UR) -- on fire.

JULY 19 *(JEREMIAH 20:9)*

Stop! Drop! And roll! Stop procrastinating. Drop your excuses. And roll with the God who saved you. You are on fire. You can't deny it. That burning, nagging uneasiness that you feel is heartburn. But Tums or Zantac won't cure it. The only way to cure it is to open your mouth and speak. David knew it. (Psalm 39:1-3) He tried to harness it. But it was too much. To hold back creates an unexplainable sorrow.

Jeremiah tried the same thing. He was upset with God. Disillusioned and disappointed, he accused God of deceiving him. He was mad because people were mocking him. So he made a decision: *"I will not make mention of Him, nor speak any more in His name."* But he couldn't do it without discomfort and neither can you. You are on fire! Stop! Drop! And roll! Stop procrastinating. (2 Corinthians 6:1,2) Drop your excuses. (Romans 1:18-22) And roll with the God who saved you. (Acts 10:38)

You Are (UR) -- allowed one giant step.

(1 PETER 2:21-25) JULY 20

On this day in 1969, Neil Armstrong became the first man to land on the moon. Armstrong's first words on the moon were,

"That's one small step for a man, one giant leap for mankind."

But long before the invention of jet propulsion, Jesus took the most important step any man will ever take. He took the first step back toward God and left us an example to follow.

We may never walk on the moon, but one day soon we will be caught up and sail out of earth's gravitational pull, past the moon, through the second heaven, to the the throne of the most high God. Now that's one giant step for mankind.

You Are (UR) -- sealed.

(2 CORINTHIANS 1:21,22) JULY 21

Seals are interesting things. They bespeak safety, security, purity, integrity, importance. Perishables are sealed for freshness. High profile papers are sealed for privacy. Jesus' tomb was sealed and guarded by soldiers. If the seal is broken on a product, we don't want it. We have more confidence in goods and services that have the appropriate agency's "Seal of Approval." We seal the deal. Things are signed, sealed and delivered. Our relationships are sealed with a kiss. Hence that most anticipated phrase: "You may kiss the bride."

But there is one important seal that you may not be aware of. *"Now he which stablisheth us with you in Christ, and hath anointed us, is God; Who hath also sealed us, and given the earnest of the Spirit in our hearts."* You are safe, secure, pure, whole, and extremely important. You are sealed.

You Are (UR) -- kept by the power of God.

JULY 22 *(1 PETER 1:3-5)*

There are many that would use this passage as a defense for the doctrine of "unconditional eternal security." *(Once saved -- always saved.)* I could argue, but it doesn't matter because, the truth is -- if you want to stay, God is promising that He will keep you.

It really is that simple. (2 Corinthians 1:12 / 11:1-3) God wants you to win. (1 Corinthians 15:57) The devil can't beat you. (Isaiah 51:12,13) You just have to decide that you want to be kept. (Deuteronomy 30:19 / Joshua 24:15)

You Are (UR) -- expecting.

JULY 23 *(ACTS 3:1-5)*

What a powerful word -- expecting. We use it to describe the condition of pregnant women. They are expecting a child. They are expecting a new life. They are expecting to continue the legacy of their forefathers. You are expecting. You are expecting miracles. You are expecting blessings. You are expecting to be healed. You are expecting to be delivered. How did you get that way? The same way those mothers did. You were impregnated by the sperma of the word. Intimacy with the omnipotent God has opened the womb of your heart and filled you with His spirit.

You, like Mary, have said, *"Behold the handmaid of the Lord: be it unto me according to thy word."* (Luke 2:26-38) Dr. Lester Sumrall once told me that the problem with the church is that *"they are on the pill."* He went on to explain that modern Christians love the excitement of church, like modern men and women love the excitement of sex, but neither wants the "discomfort" of pregnancy nor the "responsibility" of parenthood so they resist impregnation. But not you. You are expecting.

You Are (UR) -- engaged.

Now let me get this straight. It's an arranged marriage. (John 15:16) But you had the right to receive or reject the proposal. (Revelation 3:20) The bridegroom is gone away and you are not exactly sure when he's coming to get you. And the wedding date has been set, but neither you nor the bridegroom knows when it is. His dad says when. You just have to be ready. (Matthew 24:36-44)

And you've never actually seen him or his father? But you talk with him regularly and he writes wonderful letters. (1 John 5:13) In one, he said he has gone to prepare a place for you and it sounds marvelous. (John 14:1-3) Well, thank God he sent you an engagement ring -- something to seal the deal -- some earnest -- a down payment, if you will. And, con-gratulations. It sure is exciting to know you're engaged.

You Are (UR) -- clean.

It has been said that cleanliness is next to godliness. That's not in the Bible, but this is. You are clean through the word. (John 15:3) You have been washed in the blood of the Lamb. (Revelation 1:4-6) Your trans-gressions have been blotted out by God himself. (Isaiah 43:25)

You are part of the church that Jesus is looking for -- without spot or wrinkle. Ephesians 5:25-27 The truth is: Your godliness produced your cleanliness. Now you can say like Paul, **(Say it out loud!)** *"I am clean!"* Acts 18:5,6

You Are (UR) -- not ignorant of Satan's devices.

JULY 26 *(2 CORINTHIANS 2:10,11)*

The devil's game plan has not changed in six thousand years. Variations on a theme are the best he can do. He can't kill us, so he relies on people's ignorance. But you are not ignorant. It's a three part attack for a three part being. Soul shot. Body shot. Spirit shot. Go back to Genesis 3 and you've got him. He always leads with a question. *"Hath God said...?"* He always wants to know if you know the word of God. He even came at Jesus that way. (Luke 4:9-13) There is no escape. Either you know or you don't or maybe, God forbid, you don't want to know. (Hosea 4:6)

If you, like Eve, are aware of what God said, the devil moves to phase two. *"You shall not surely die."* Okay, God said it, but that can't be what he meant. Most people, like Eve, drop the ball here. Silent contemplation of proposed possibilities kills Christians every day. **Say it out loud!** *"If I regard iniquity in my heart, the Lord will not hear me."* (Psalm 66:18)

Odd how the lie uses God's exact words. *"You shall not surely die."* There are entire denominations divided over the literal infallibility of the word of God. They are divided because those denominations are made up of individuals who are divided, within themselves, over the literal infallibility of the word of God. And they all defend their positions using -- you guessed it -- the word of God.

Finally, Satan moves in for the kill. *"For God doth know...."* Suddenly, God is a deceitful adversary who does not have your best interests at heart. But wait. That's the devil I just described. (1 Peter 5:8,9) It's an old game. But you are not ignorant.

You know that *"the thief cometh not but for to steal, and to kill, and to destroy."* (John 10:10) You know that *"he was a murderer from the beginning, and abode not in the truth, because there is no truth in him. When he speaks a lie he speaks of his own: for he is a liar and the father of it."* (John 8:44) You know he fell like lightning and that you have *"power to tread on serpents and scorpions and over all the power of the enemy."* (Luke 10:17-19) You are not ignorant at all. **Say it out loud!** I am not ignorant of Satan's devices!

You Are (UR) -- doing...?

(1 Corinthians 4:3-5) July 27

People keep asking me: *"So, how are you doing?"* Or, *"How's the church?"* I realize that most of them mean well and really care about my well being. The rest are just being sociable. But I'm beginning to question my answers. I mean, if things are not going so well, I don't want to burden them with my bellyaching. And I certainly don't want to 'sound' discouraged. If things are going great, I don't want to appear braggadocio or, God forbid, overly confident. But the fact is, I don't really know how I'm doing. Do you?

I know the things I'm doing. And I know how I feel about my situation or condition when I'm asked. But my feelings shift like the wind and simply must not be trusted. And the things I'm doing vary from the sublime to the ridiculous. I'm not so sure I always know which is which. So when asked how I'm doing I think -- and may begin to say: Compared to what?

My church is larger than some and smaller than others. I have more money than some and less than others. I am not sick, but I'm no poster child for physical fitness either. How am I doing? Paul said, *"judge nothing before the time."* Amen brother! It's too soon to tell. {See 9/12}

You Are (UR) -- called and chosen and faithful.

(Revelation 17:14) July 28

Many are called but few are chosen. (Matthew 20:16 & 22:14) What may be truer still is that many are called but few choose to go. But you are with Jesus. *"And they that are with him are called and chosen and faithful."* You are the called according to his purpose. (Romans 8:28) He chose you. (John 15:16) And you are filled with the faith of the God of all creation. (Romans 12:3)

You Are (UR) -- alive.

JULY 29 *(ECCLESIASTES 9:4-6)*

Great things can happen for you today.
You are alive.
Your aches and pains can go away.
You are alive.
You can find the resources to meet your needs.
You can reap a harvest from forgotten seeds.
You can follow up on red hot leads.
You are alive.

You can release the grudge that you've been holding.
You are alive.
You can throw out things that are dead and molding.
You are alive.
You can be forgiven all your sin.
You can get back up and try again.
The game's not over and you can win.
You are alive.

You Are (UR) -- on the road to perfection.

JULY 30 *(PSALM 138:8)*

God does not stutter when he says, *"Be perfect."* (Matthew 5:48) But people are quick to remind us that we are not perfect. Our imperfections pop up moment to moment. (Pay no attention to typos in this piece.;-) Paul acknowledged: *"Not as though I had already attained, either were already perfect: but I follow after, if that I may apprehend that for which also I am apprehended of Christ Jesus."* (Philippians 3:12) Jesus caught you and you are trying to catch what He caught you for. But praise God, you are not on your own. Everything that concerns you -- concerns Him. Why? Because He made you. He made you perfect and He will not forsake you. The Lord will perfect that which concerns you. He won't forsake the work of His hands -- and that's you.

You Are (UR) -- cursed with a curse.

{This is designed specifically for people with persistent or recurring problems.}

(MALACHI 3 ESP. VS 9) JULY 31

I know it doesn't sound too encouraging, but this is a very real possibility and acknowledging it is the first step toward removing it. There are times in our lives when we face obstacles that we just can't seem to get around. We work, strategize, struggle and even pray, but the thing remains or returns. Remember the man with the demon possessed son in Mark 9:14-29? Only fasting would get the job done.

In such cases, the Bible makes it clear that because of pride, it may actually be God that is resisting us. (James 4:6) Or worse; it may be a curse. (Malachi 3 especially vs. 9) Either way, it's difficult to see and almost impossible to fix on your own, especially while you are caught in the rhythm of your routine. Now that you know, however, you can repent and change the behavior that caused it. (Proverbs 26:2) Now that's encouraging. *(See 11/15 for a practical example.)*

You Are (UR) -- temperate in all things.

(1 CORINTHIANS 9:25) AUGUST 1

Say it out loud! I am temperate in all things. I am striving to obtain an incorruptible crown and I must be in control of the atmosphere around me. (Psalm 112 esp. vs. 7) Moderation is my motto. (Philippians 4:4-8) I am a thermostat -- not a thermometer. While others complain of how things are and vacillate through a life of situational conversation and ethics, I have the nature of the most high.

I have escaped the corruption that is in the world through lust. (2 Peter 1:1-4) He changes not. (Malachi 3:6) And I, through him, am the same, yesterday and today and forever. (Hebrews 13:8) In me, through Him, there is no variableness nor shadow of turning. (James 1:16,17) I am at high noon -- peak performance -- at all times. I am pressing toward the mark for the prize of the high calling of God in Christ Jesus. (Philippians 3:13,14) I am temperate in all things.

You Are (UR) -- going to die.

AUGUST 2 *(2 KINGS 20:1-7)*

I know it sounds like I'm on some sort of doom loop, but bear with me for a minute. That declaration is nothing compared to what Isaiah told Hezekiah. When Nathan exposed David, David was so aware of the magnitude of his sin, he sentenced himself to death. (2 Samuel 12:1-13) And Jairus' servants admonished him, *"Why troublest thou the master any longer? Thy daughter is dead."* (Mark 5:21-42) All these men recovered from the terminal declarations of people who spoke with un-questionable authority.

Your doctor told you to get your house in order. Your illness is terminal. Your boss just fired you and the review board has snatched your creden-tials. You've been disgraced -- defrocked -- disbarred. Your son, your daughter, your marriage, your _____ is dead.

"Be not afraid," Jesus said to Jairus, *"only believe."* Jairus dined with a living daughter that day. David repented and Nathan refuted the king's personal death sentence. Hezekiah turned his face to the wall and begged. He humbled himself in the sight of the Lord and prayed. (2 Chronicles 7:14 / James 4:6-10) And the same God that sent Isaiah to tell him he was going to die, turned Isaiah around and sent him back with the good news: *"I have heard thy prayer, I have seen thy tears: behold I will heal thee: on the third day thou shalt go up unto the house of the Lord. And I will add unto thy days fifteen years...."*

Death doesn't have to be a death sentence. Since the beginning, God has called those things which be not as though they were. When the earth was without form and void and darkness was upon the face of the deep, the spirit of God moved upon the face of the waters and God said: *"Let there be light."* The same God said to a decaying Lazarus: *"Come forth!"* And He calls you forth today.

You Are (UR) -- built up.

Exercise is all the rage and I guess it has its place. People run, work out and train. And the scriptures say it *"profiteth little."* (1 Timothy 4:8) That's not to say don't do it. Little beats none. But you are a three part being. Soul, Spirit and Body. (1 Thessalonians 5:23) While others expand their minds and stretch their bodies, you have the added benefit of being built up on your most holy faith -- praying in the Holy Ghost. The apostles considered it essential to the Christian experience.

Paul asked the disciples at Ephesus: *"Have you received the Holy Ghost since you believed?"* When they replied, *"We have not so much as heard whether there be any Holy Ghost,"* he wanted to know if they were saved. *"Unto what then were you baptized?"* he asked. Sure enough, they had undergone John's baptism but had yet to hear of Jesus. He led them to Christ and immersed them in water and laid hands on them. *"The Holy Ghost came on them: and they spake with other tongues and prophesied."* Now that's what I call a full work-out. Soul, Body, and Spirit.

You Are (UR) -- illuminated.

Say it out loud! My candle is lit and the glory of the Lord is shining brightly in, on, and through me. I can see. I am no longer groping about in gross darkness. What's wrong is being exposed and the right way is clearly evident. I am walking in the light. Some folks may not like it. Evil prefers darkness. But I have cast off the works of darkness and I daily put on the armour of light. My troubles may seem magnified now that I can see. I know it's simply because the devil would love to discourage me. But I am illuminated. I am fired up -- turned on -- tuned in -- and fully focused. It doesn't matter where I've been, now that I see where I'm going.

You Are (UR) -- a walking word.

AUGUST 5 *(GENESIS 1:26-28)*

You are the marvelous manifestation of an expressed idea -- straight from the heart of God. You are what he had in mind when he said, *"let us make man."* You are made in his image and after his likeness. And believe it or not, you have dominion over the fish of the sea, and over the fowl of the air, and over the cattle, and over all the earth, and over every creeping thing that creepeth upon the earth. You are blessed and full of fruit. Multiplying, replenishing, subjective dominion is what God expects from you, His walking word. (Jeremiah 29:11)

"For as the rain comes down and the snow from heaven, and returneth not thither, but watereth the earth, and maketh it bring forth and bud, that it may give seed to the sower and bread to the eater:" So shall you be that goeth forth out of God's mouth: you shall not return to him void, but you shall accomplish that which He pleases, and you shall prosper in the thing whereto He sent you. (Isaiah 55:10,11)

You Are (UR) -- following your confession.

AUGUST 6 *(ROMANS 10:8-10)*

Imagine a running back headed down-field. He begins to point out blocks as the crowd cheers. Teammates begin to take out opponents and the gap widens. He sees daylight and smells the end zone. Wouldn't it be peculiar if he turned the other way and started running back into trouble?

The words you speak express what you believe and declare the path you intend to follow. Angels respond. (Hebrews 1:13,14) Devils respond. (Revelation 12:10-12) All of creation waits to respond. (Romans 8:18,19) It confuses them when you go in a different direction. And you find a much tougher path to follow. **Say it out loud!** I am following my confession!

You Are (UR) -- just getting started.

(REVELATION 7:9-17) AUGUST 7

I look forward to the day I will stand before the throne amidst the innu-merable multitude in a robe made white by the blood of the Lamb. My voice cries out in anticipation, praising the one who was and is and is to come. But in the midst of my worship, I become keenly aware that the yearning, though unavoidable, is oddly unnecessary.

I need not wait or anticipate, for I am already here. I am seated in heav-enly places, in Christ Jesus. As He is, so am I in this world. Time is transcended. Space is no more. Difficulty and death are squarely cir-cumvented. Eons like seconds soar.

He is Alpha and Omega, the beginning and the ending and I am in Him. And just when I think my life is ending, I can see I have just begun.

Amen! Blessing and glory and wisdom, and thanksgiving, and honor, and power, and might be unto our God for ever and ever. Amen! I can say as He has said: *"Before anything was, I AM."*

You Are (UR) -- fighting for something grand.

(NEHEMIAH 4:1-14) AUGUST 8

You may get a little weary and trouble may be on every side. But remem-ber: You are fighting for your brethren, your sons, and your daughters, your wives and your houses *(your legacy)*. So don't neglect your vision and don't forget your God. He is great and terrible and you are aligned with His righteous cause. Shout for joy and be glad and say continually: *"Let the Lord be magnified, which hath pleasure in the prosperity of his servant."* (Psalm 35:27) You are fighting for something grand.

You Are (UR) -- a contender.

AUGUST 9 *(JUDE 3)*

The reigning champs of this world, Adam & Eve, relinquished their title and with it, all the privileges of dominion over the earth. Satan *(Lucifer, Beelzebub, That Old Serpent The Devil)* reigned as the prince of the power of the air with power over the earth as well. Then Jesus *(The King of kings. The Lord of lords. The Lily of the Valley. The Bright and Morning Star. That Wheel in the Middle of a Wheel. Alpha and Omega. He who Is and Was and Is to come)* came.

He defeated the devil. He took the keys of death, hell and the grave. And he has returned to us the right to reign with him as heirs -- heirs of God and joint heirs with Christ. But not without a fight. We must contend for the faith that was once delivered to the saints. We must overcome Satan by the blood of the Lamb and the word of our testimony. And we must love not our lives even unto the death. Paul said, *"I have fought a good fight."* (2 Timothy 4:7) Let us say the same thing. Fight back! You are a contender.

You Are (UR) -- a triple threat.

AUGUST 10 *(1 THESSALONIANS 5:23)*

In his benediction to the church at Thessalonica, Paul prayed an important prayer for you. He asked that the very God of peace would *"sanctify you wholly."* This is holistic thinking at its best. He then identified your three parts: spirit, soul and body. You serve a triune God -- Father, Son and Holy Ghost. And you are a three part being. The devil knows this and attacks on all three levels, often pitting one force against another within you. He even goes so far as to cause confusion about who "you" really are. But here are three indisputable truths. The word of God is clear. The devil is defeated. And Jesus is Lord.

You Are (UR) -- a triple threat.

(1 Thessalonians 5:23) AUGUST 11

You are a living soul. When God blew the breath of life *(the pneuma -- His Spirit)* into Adam's nostrils, he became something. He became a living soul. It is the miraculous mingling of Spirit upon spirit in flesh. Suddenly, Adam was like God. He had creative power and authorized dominion. He could carry out God's inspired dream.

Meanwhile, back at the tree of the knowledge of good and evil, the devil was at work on that which challenges the soul *(the mind, the emotions and the will)*. He was asking questions, assuming answers and making accusations. *"Hath God said...? You shall not surely die? For God doth know...."* And man became a dead soul.

Four thousand years later, Jesus shed his blood to forgive and cleanse us. He restoreth our souls. And while the disciples were hiding to save their "so called" lives, He breathed *(pneuma-ed)* on them saying, *"receive ye the Holy Ghost,"* and again we became -- living souls. You are a part of that lineage, so be prepared for Satan's questions, assumed answers and hurled accusations. Hit him with a 1,2 - 3 combination. God said it. He meant it. And He's here, with me, to represent it. You are a triple threat.

You Are (UR) -- a triple threat.

(1 Thessalonians 5:23) AUGUST 12

You have a spirit. (Proverbs 20:27) God calls your spirit his candle -- His pilot light. Unfortunately, the flame that lights it can be light or dark. God's or the devil's (Matthew 6:22,23) The distinction between the two means life or death. And the soulish man gets to choose. *"Choose life,"* God says. (Deuteronomy 30:19) *"Choose life, that both thou and thy seed may live: That thou mayest love the Lord thy God, and that thou mayest cleave unto him: for he is thy life, and the length of thy days: that thou mayest dwell in the land which the Lord sware unto thy fathers, to Abraham, to Isaac, and to Jacob, to give them."*

You Are (UR) -- a triple threat.

AUGUST 13 *(1 THESSALONIANS 5:23)*

You are also flesh. (Genesis 6:3) On September 11, 2001, thousands of souls slipped into eternity. It actually happens every day. Old age, Hunger, Disease, Crime, War, etc..., etc..., ad infinitum. Some of them know Jesus and stand before his throne. Others do not and await judgment and damnation. In this case, however, we saw it, en masse, on television. And we were left with an unimaginable number of dead bodies. For weeks we waited, watched or worked through mountains of charred, mangled flesh. And at the end of the day, we found we had to make some pivotal choices. (Matthew 24:12)

Attacks on the flesh always challenge the soulish man to choose between the immediate comfort and protection of the flesh and the eternal commandment and promise of the Spirit. (Job 36:21 / 2 Corinthians 4:13-18) It is here the questions, assumptions and accusations fly. *"Hath God said? You shall not surely die? For God doth know...."* Don't make Adam & Eve's mistake. (Genesis 3:1-19) Remember Lot's wife. (Genesis 19:1-26) Go not in the way of Cain nor run after the error of Balaam. (Genesis 4/22/23/24) If your flesh is under attack and you are grappling with impossible choices, refer to Galatians 2:20 / 5:13-26 / 6:7-9, Romans 7 / 8:1-14. And never ever forget: You are a triple threat!

You Are (UR) -- a triple threat.

AUGUST 14 *(1 THESSALONIANS 5:23)*

You are a three-fold-cord that is not easily broken. (Ecclesiastes 4:9-12) You are a soul. You have a spirit. And you live in a body. You worship the Father in the name of the Son and you are led by the Holy Spirit. Your God reigns in heaven, earth and under the earth. And you are born of the Spirit and the water and washed in the blood. And these three agree in one. (1 John 5:7) Your angry enemies marvel as you are joined in the fire that they condemned you to by the fourth man -- the Son of God. (Daniel 3) **Say it out loud!** I am a triple threat!

You Are (UR) -- a man after God's own heart.

(ACTS 13:22) AUGUST 15

I used to read this description of David, king of Israel, and think: *"David was God's kind of guy."* Then I spent three glorious days on Oak Island at a retreat with the men of Christ Community Church and I got a revelation. These guys are actually *after* God's heart. They are pursuing it. They are trying desperately to get to it. They have committed themselves to God like David's friend Jonathan's armourbearer did to him. *"Do all that is in thine heart,"* they have said to God. *"Turn thee; behold, I am with thee according to thy heart."*

It's so obvious now. *"But without faith it is impossible to please him for he that cometh to God must believe that he is and that he is a rewarder of them that diligently seek him."* (Hebrews 11:6) We all must need be *after* God's heart.

You Are (UR) -- prepared for takeoff.

(2 TIMOTHY 4:7,8) AUGUST 16

Jesus went up with a shout in a cloud
He'll come back in the very same way (Acts 1:10-12)
He's coming to get us He'll call us out loud (1 Thessalonians 4:16-18)
His return could occur any day (Luke 12:40)

Lay aside every weight and your burden of sin
You've got to be light for the flight (Hebrews 12:1,2)
He only requires that you be born again (John 3:3-7)
And walk not in darkness, but light (1 John 1:5-7 / Romans 13:11,12)

You Are (UR) -- not a sinner.

AUGUST 17 *(1 TIMOTHY 1:15)*

"I'm just an old sinner saved by grace."

I hear people say it all the time and I thought I had learned to ignore it as so much misplaced religion. But this is serious business folks. You have entered the realm of mutual exclusivity. You are either saved or you are a sinner. You can't be both.

Paul's comments in his letter to Timothy must not be misunderstood. He is not claiming to be the current *"chief of sinners."* He is claiming to be the chief recipient of the forgiveness that Jesus provided to save a sinful world. If you're not convinced, look at one of Paul's other comments on the subject.

"What shall we say then? Shall we continue in sin, that grace may abound? God forbid. How shall we, that are dead to sin, live any longer therein?" (Romans 6:1,2) This is a man who abhorred sin and all its accoutrements.

Consider the response of the blind boy Jesus healed to the Pharisees who questioned his healing: *"Now we know that God heareth not sinners:"* (John 9:31) John Mark reminded us: *"If we confess our sins, he is faithful and just to forgive us our sins and cleanse us from all unrighteousness."* (1 John 1:9) We are further admonished to *"sin not."* (1 John 2:1,2) And we are warned that everyone who commits sin *(continues in sin - hence a sinner)* is *"of the devil."* And Jesus came to *"destroy the works of the devil."* (1 John 3:8)

Yes, we were all born sinners. Surely, we have all sinned and come short of the glory of God. And there is no doubt that we all have the potential to sin again. But Jesus is our advocate in the event that we do. Our sins have been forgiven and our transgressions are blotted out. We are new creatures in Christ Jesus. Our names are written in the Lamb's Book of Life. And we who name the name of Christ are no longer sinners!

For once in your life, agree with God and not your tradition. You are not a sinner. You are the righteousness of God in Christ Jesus.

You Are (UR) -- a forecaster.

(MARK 4:35-41) AUGUST 18

The prognosticators seem fascinated by their ability to eloquently describe horror. They give storms and diseases fabulous names and predict destruction with prize winning prose. But they are not forecasters. They can only say what they see. It is your agreement that gives their folly force. At the end of the day -- they will see what you say.

"Master, carest thou not that we perish?" The disciples cried as the storm raged. *"Peace! Be still,"* Jesus commanded. And the storm ceased, causing incredulous inquiry. *"What manner of man is this?"* He is the prototype for you and me. He is a man of faith and so are you. *"Greater works than these shall ye do because I go unto my father."* (John 14:12) That's what Jesus said. So speak to the storm in your life and it ought to obey you. Let others report the weather. You proclaim the whether.

You Are (UR) -- enriched.

(1 CORINTHIANS 1:4-11) AUGUST 19

In everything, you are enriched by God in all utterance and knowledge. The testimony of Christ, which is the Spirit of prophecy, is being confirmed in you daily. Surely you come behind in no gift. Paul said this to the church at Corinth and we walk in the same blessing. Along with that blessing comes a word of warning. He begged them not to be contentious and divisive, and we must be wary of the same pitfalls. (1 Timothy 6:17-19) With all of our riches -- *naturally or spiritually* -- we must be careful not to get high-minded or overly confident. We must always trust in God who has given us richly all things to enjoy. Good should always be the aim of our efforts, and giving must be the habit of our heart. Then and only then will God trust us with the true riches and we can say like Paul: *"I know both how to be abased, and I know how to abound: every where and in all things I am instructed both to be full and to be hungry, both to abound and to suffer need. I can do all things through Christ which strengtheneth me."* (Philippians 4:12,13)

You Are (UR) -- called to obedience.

AUGUST 20 *(1 SAMUEL 15:22,23)*

God's fundamental demands on our lives are relatively simple. *"Thou shalt love the Lord thy God with all thy heart, and with all thy soul, and with all thy strength, and all thy mind; and thy neighbor as thyself."* (Luke 10:25-27) Okay -- He gets a little more specific. *"You must be born again."* (John 3:1-7) *"Go into all the world and preach the gospel."* (Mark 16:15-20) *"Pray without ceasing."* (1 Thessalonians 5:17) *"Give and it shall be given unto you."* (Matthew 6:38) And then, of course, we are admonished to *"work out our own salvation with fear and trembling."* (Philippians 2:12,13) But none of the above is difficult to decipher or do when you love *(fear, obey, worship)* God.

The problems start when our hearts get divided and we choose the creation over the creator. Suddenly our lives are filled with sacrifices, offerings, rituals and prayers for God to deliver us from things we got into because we feared man. *The recipe for life is simple. And the principal ingredient is for you to be obedient.

You Are (UR) -- privileged.

AUGUST 21 *(PSALM 149)*

You can praise God and punish the devil. You can sing a new song and worship with the saints. You can rejoice in the God that made you and be filled with joy in your King. You can dance and express your praise with instruments. You have the comfort of knowing that God is pleased with you and replaces your shame and ashes with beauty and glory. You can shout on your bed and speak highly of your God. You are meek but not weak. You praise in power. You carry a song and a sword. The new song in your mouth will be *(seen)* and strike fear in the heart of the devil himself. And your words bind and loose and declare the will of God in the earth. It is an honor that not everyone has. You are privileged.

You Are (UR) -- not what you used to be.

(EPHESIANS 2) AUGUST 22

I found out the hard way, that all personal computer programs run through *"available memory."* The more DRAM or RAM (Dynamic Random Access Memory) you have, the faster your computer is. That is, provided the RAM is available and uncorrupted. A bad piece of memory turns your laptop into a flashing, high-priced paperweight.

Your life is lived through available, uncorrupted memory, too. If your mind is cluttered, damaged or even unreasonably *"secured"* by what you *"used to be,"* you cannot process present programs and applications properly. Sooner or later you are going to freeze, crash or shut down. That's why you need to be *"saved"* and your memory *"backed up"* regularly. Hopefully you recognize these techno-geek terms:

> **Saved:** Get your life out of temporary memory into a preserved place of supernatural reality.

> **Backed Up:** Clean out your memory so that you keep as much of it readily available as possible. The blood of Christ and the word of God are the best cleansers.

> **Store:** Keep old victories in convenient places so that you can access them as needed and trash everything else.

You are the most powerful processor of information ever created. Keep it that way. And always remember: You are not what you used to be. You are what you are by the grace of God.

"These are the days for strong men to courageously expose wrong."

Adam Clayton Powell, Jr.

You Are (UR) -- too sensitive.

AUGUST 23 *(ECCLESIASTES 7:21,22)*

Words are important, there is no denying. Sometimes, however, we make them far more important than they really are. I realize that out of the abundance of the heart, the mouth speaks. (Matthew 12:34) But did you know that the heart is deceitful above all things and desperately wicked? The scriptures ask, *"who can know it?"* (Jeremiah 17:9) Perhaps you have had some unkind things said to you or about you. It hurts worst coming from those closest to you. The devil knows this and plays it like an instrument. So before you take it to heart, consider this. Some words were not meant for your hearing. And some words, spoken in anger, haste, or ignorance *(heard or not)*, were simply not meant.

You remember the time you told your mother you hated her? You did not and do not hate your mother. You hated the fact that she wouldn't let you do what you wanted to do. You hated the fact that no matter what you did, she always knew what you were doing. And now you hate the fact that you are doing exactly what she did, which is something you said you'd never do. Now you are getting it back, in spades, from your kids and you hate that too.

Have you considered the fact that you are getting these profoundly hurtful ejaculations from people who have the emotional maturity and/or the spiritual depth of a butter bean? Lighten up. You are too sensitive.

You Are (UR) -- it.

AUGUST 24 *(COLOSSIANS 3:1-4)*

When we were kids, we played hide and seek. Now the game is our reality. Your life is hid with Christ in God. And you are seeking those things which are above. And the devil is a rotten egg.

You Are (UR) -- the word made flesh.

(JOHN 1:12-14) AUGUST 25

You are a manifestation of God's desire. You are what He had in mind when he said; *"let us make man."* You are a supernatural idea with natural applications. You are the word made flesh. Hebrews 11:3 teaches that *"through faith we understand that the worlds were framed by the word of God, so that things which are seen were not made of things which do appear."* You are just one of those things. Romans 4:17 declares that God *"calls those things which be not as though they were."* You are simply heeding the call.

The first Adam interrupted God's plan by not believing that God meant what He said and by allowing Satan to make him suspect God. But when Jesus, the last Adam, became flesh and walked among us, He succeeded where the first Adam failed. Yes, the horror of being forsaken came. But it was too late. Jesus had already decided and declared: *"Not my will be done, but thine."*

Jesus knew that it is God that dwells in us, both to will and to do of His good pleasure. (Philippians 2:12,13) He believed that it is the will of God that none should perish. (2 Peter 3:9) He was committed to the concept that God takes pleasure in the prosperity of His servant. (Psalm 35:27) He benefitted from the fact that God wishes above all things thou mayest prosper and be in health even as your soul prospers. And if you would simply agree with Him, He would work that and more out in you. God is a spirit. You are the word made flesh.

You Are (UR) -- adopted.

(ROMANS 8:14,15) AUGUST 26

Jesus is the only begotten son of God. (1 John 4:9) The rest of us are adopted. Other children *(and sometimes our own minds)* may try to be-little us or make us feel inferior. But then Daddy (Abba) says: *"You have not chosen me, but I have chosen you..."* (John 15:16) and all is well.

You Are (UR) -- asking amiss.

AUGUST 27 *(JAMES 4:1-3)*

Not very encouraging? Well, at least you know what to work on. Charles Grandison Finney, one of the greatest evangelists America has ever known, wrote in his autobiography of a Mr. B___, in whose home he was staying while evangelizing upstate New York.

"One day as I came down from my room and was going out to call on some inquirers, I met Mr. B__ in the hall." He said to me, *"Mr. Finney, what would you think of a man who was praying week after week for the Holy Spirit (insert any object of your prayer life here) and could get no answer?"* *"I replied,"* said Finney, "that I would think he was praying from false motives."

"But from what motives," said Mr. B__, *"should a man pray? If he wants to be happy, is that a false motive?"* Finney replied, *"Satan might pray with as good a motive as that."* And then Finney quoted the words of the Psalmist: (Psalm 51) *" 'Uphold me with thy free spirit. Then will I teach transgressors thy ways, and sinners shall be converted unto thee. See?"* Finney said, *"the Psalmist did not pray for the Holy Spirit that he might be happy, but that he might be useful and that sinners might be converted to Christ."*

You Are (UR) -- what you think you are.

AUGUST 28 *(PROVERBS 23:7)*

Brush your teeth. Shower. Prepare your clothing. Dress. Do your hair. Apply make up and fragrance. Straighten your tie. Now look in the mirror. All of this is subject to change the minute you open your mouth. If you want what you've worked so hard to create to translate accurately, you must adjust your heart *(soul, mind, emotions and will)*. (Matthew 12:34) Because as a man thinks in his heart -- so is he.

You Are (UR) -- out of order.

(1 CORINTHIANS 14:40) AUGUST 29

Look at any dictionary and you will discover this simple truth. *Go* comes before *God* and *God* comes before *Good.* So why are so many people waiting for a move of God before they make a move of their own? He says: *"Go ye therefore." "Take up thy bed and walk." "Come." "Arise."* The miracles occurred after the action began. Even the four lepers of 2 Kings 7 surmised; *"Why sit we here until we die?"* And Jonathan understood, saying: *"Come, and let us go over unto the garrison of these uncircumcised: it may be that the Lord will work for us:"* (1 Samuel 14:6) Movement before miracles. *Go* before *God.*

But even for those who go, there is often the question of direction in pursuit of perfection. There are so many who are going, but they refuse to go to God because they don't feel *"good enough"* yet. How absurd. Jesus said, *"There is none good but one, that is, God."* (Mark 10:17,18) You will never be clean enough to please him. On your best day, your righteousness is as filthy rags. (Isaiah 64:6) If you won't read the Bible - read the dictionary. Get up and Go to God and you will be made Good.

You Are (UR) -- in the kingdom for such a time as this.

(ESTHER 4:14) AUGUST 30

Esther found herself in a curious position. All the grace and favour she had obtained was neither random nor arbitrary. God had put her in position for a purpose. She had eaten and was full. Now it was time to bless the Lord. (Deuteronomy 8:10) She had danced. It was time to pay the band. You are where you are right now by God's grace. Sure, you worked hard. And yes, you are talented. But there is no accounting for the fact that the powers that be, like you. You have obtained favour from the Lord. Sooner or later He will call on you to use your influence, position and power for his purpose.

You Are (UR) -- my friend.

AUGUST 31 *(PROVERBS 18:24)*

I once heard Pastor Tommy Barnett say that he could befriend anyone he wanted to, with or without their permission. He simply had to decide to include them in his *"circle of love."* From that perspective, however, the title of this message would better be: I am your friend.

Jesus said: *"Ye are my friends, if ye do whatsoever I command you."* We know that Jesus is our friend - a friend who sticks closer than a brother. He has commended his love toward us, in that, while we were yet sinners, Christ died for us. (Romans 5:8) So the real question is: Are you his friend?

You Are (UR) -- an EncourageMINT.

SEPTEMBER 1 *(2 CHRON. 31:4,5)*

You are a source of great courage and inspiration for those who inspire you. It begins with your *"Amen!"* The man of God is encouraged when the people of God agree -- not with him -- with God. Paul knew that the unlearned cannot say *"Amen"* because they are void of understanding. (1 Corinthians 14:16) Hosea knew that God's people perish because they reject knowledge and strive with the priests. (Hosea 4:1-6) But when there is agreement, heaven moves. (Genesis 11:1-6 / Matthew 18:18,19)

There is great comfort for those who preach in the mingled faith of those who receive. (Romans 1:8-12) So as you learn the word and stand under authority, your expressed "Amen" will encourage those who encourage you. You are an EncourageMINT.

You Are (UR) -- an EncourageMINT.

(1 SAMUEL 14:6,7) SEPTEMBER 2

Your *"Amen"* is important. But God is looking for A Man. (Ezekiel 22:30) So are most men of God. The average man of God has no delusions about capturing the hearts of great crowds. Even Jesus lost six thousand in one day and turned to ask the twelve, *"will you also go away?"* (John 6:66) But you don't have to follow the crowd.

You are an encouragement when you add your alignment to your agreement. Say and do as the armourbearer did. *"Do all that is in thine heart,"* he said to Jonathan; *"turn thee; behold, I am with thee according to your heart."* Your pastor could change the world with one such saint, for where two or more are in agreement, I AM is in the midst. The devil knows this too, so he does all he can to make you a source of grief rather than joy. (Hebrews 13:17) Don't think super spiritual. Think common place. Think about being in place - on time - with a willing heart. You are an EncourageMINT.

You Are (UR) -- an EncourageMINT.

(1 SAMUEL 30:1-6) SEPTEMBER 3

King David had to encourage himself in the Lord his God. When he and his men returned from their mercenary duties, they found their camp destroyed and their wives, children, and possessions missing. The men had lost something of value and they blamed David in their despair. Remember, they were in distress, in debt and discontented to begin with. (1 Samuel 22:2) But you can find strength in the midst of your trouble and encourage those around you by mingling your setbacks and their accompanying afflictions with joy and liberality. (2 Corinthians 8:1-5) Rather than focusing on your losses, you can encourage yourself and those who encourage you by giving. (2 Chronicles 31:4,5) You are an EncourageMINT.

You Are (UR) -- an EncourageMINT.

SEPTEMBER 4 *(JOSHUA 1:1-9)*

God IS with you wherever you go. How can you be anything but encouraged and consequently an EncourageMINT? All things are yours except the battle, which is the Lord's. (1 Corinthians 3:16-23 / 2 Chronicles 20:14,15) No weapon formed against you shall prosper. (Isaiah 54:17) He has given you power to tread on serpents and scorpions and over all the power of the enemy. (Luke 10:19) He will never leave you nor forsake you. (Hebrews 13:5,6) And He has promised to perfect that which concerns you. (Psalm 138:8) *"Be strong and of a good courage"* was not a request. It was a command. And make no mistake -- God will be very upset if you don't trust him. (See Isaiah 52:12,13) **Say it out loud!** I am an EncourageMINT!!

You Are (UR) -- declaring your worth.

SEPTEMBER 5 *(PROVERBS 14:23)*

Today is Labor Day. I have always found it amusing *(pronounced confusing)* that we celebrate it by not working. But then again, the concept of work seems to confuse people, too. First of all, work did not come as a result of the sin of Adam. Adam had a job before he sinned. Work was never intended as a punishment, but as a glorious opportunity to co-labor with our creator. You can read Adam and Eve's job description in Genesis 1:26-28.

Secondly, remuneration for labor is determined by the heart and the mouth not the head, the back, or the feet. People think, *"If I learn more, work harder and/or do something more 'important,' I should have more."* Meanwhile, God says, *"In all labor there is profit. But the talk of the lips tendeth only to penury."* Work on this this Labor Day. What you believe, will control what you say. And what you say will always determine your pay. (Genesis 30:25-43 / Haggai 1:1-15 / Matthew 20:1-16)

You Are (UR) -- going to try again.

(LUKE 5:1-11) SEPTEMBER 6

If this doesn't apply to you right now, it applies to someone you know and it will probably apply to you sooner or later. All who endeavor to do anything, experience failure from time to time. Along with failure comes frustration and sometimes, despair. But most of all, there are questions. *"Am I in the right place?" "Am I doing the right thing?" "Is something wrong with me?"* These are the nagging naysayers that accompany failure. And they didn't begin with you.

Peter and his associates were cleaning up after a not-so-successful day of fishing, when Jesus, the son of God, the God who is Love, which never fails, appeared. *"May I use your boat to preach the gospel?"* He inquired. *"Why not, I'm done for the day,"* Peter probably responded.

There are things you have that lay dormant and unused when you are not at work. Perhaps Jesus could use them to preach the gospel. Your car. Your house. Your business. Your talent.

Never forget: Things done for the King are recorded, remembered and rewarded. (Esther 2:21-23)

When Jesus finished, he challenged Peter to try again. *"Launch out into the deep, and let down your nets for a draught."* The mandate was and is: Make a full commitment. Go all the way back out and let all of your nets down. This time you are going to succeed. But failure has a way of creating resistance to hope.

"Master, we have toiled all the night and have taken nothing, nevertheless at thy word I will let down the net." Only one net Peter? The word was nets not net. Last night your problem was not enough. But today your problem may be too much. Because today you are going to try again. And today you are going to succeed.

You Are (UR) -- going down.

SEPTEMBER 7 *(ACTS 8)*

Philip went down to the city of Samaria and preached Christ to them. Not many people are interested in going down nowadays. Everybody wants to move up. We want to associate with others who are moving up. But Philip went down. And when he did, the people listened to what he had to say because God approved his words with miracles. People got saved and healed and there was great joy in that city.

Many believe that the Samaritans were prepared for Philip's arrival by the woman at the well of John 4. She had met the savior and gone home to tell all, *"Come, see a man...is not this the Christ?"* This happened because Jesus felt He too, *"must needs go* (down) *through Samaria."*

Your decision to go in the name of Jesus will always bring great joy. It may seem like you're going down, but the word will bring people up. *"Go ye therefore and teach all nations."* (Matthew 28:18-20) *"Go into all the world and preach the gospel to every creature."* (Mark 16:15-20)

You Are (UR) -- holding things up.

SEPTEMBER 8 *(EXODUS 17:8-14)*

Joshua was in the valley of Rephidim doing battle with the Amalekites. Moses was on the hill with Aaron and Hur praying. When Moses held up the rod of God, Joshua prevailed. When the rod came down, Amalek prevailed. Moses tried to keep his arms up but he grew weary. Aaron and Hur, seeing the connection, made a decision.

Now, they could have blamed Moses for not being strong enough. They could have murmured and complained and accused him of getting them into this predicament in the first place, like David's men in 1 Samuel 30, but they didn't. They sat Moses on a rock, stood on either side of him and held up his hands. How about you? **Say it out loud!** I am holding things up.

You Are (UR) -- the head and not the tail.

When God said this to Abram, he was describing that which had not yet been. He was calling those things which be not as though they were. I think we forget that Abraham was the first of his kind. Both Jew and Gentile, he embodied a church unborn. Abram walked by faith. Abram walked with God. Abram became Abraham, the man that God declared he was.

Paul posed the question to the Romans; *"What shall we say then that Abraham our father, as pertaining to the flesh hath found?"* What, indeed? How is it that this nomad with no children could come to know the one God who could take him from the middle of nowhere to be known of all? Abram did the one thing that so many of us struggle with. He took God at his word. He believed God. (Mark 9:23)

It took him almost fifteen years to do it -- but he did. *(God first spoke to Abram when he was seventy-five. Ishmael was born when Abram was eighty-six, and Abram became Abraham at ninety. New name -- New man. See Genesis 12:1-4 / 16:15,16 / 17:1-4 / 1 Samuel 10:6)* It took Sarah another nine years and a visit from God himself to get past the humor of it all.

Time, trials, vicissitudes, and visitations notwithstanding, Abraham finally decided that God's word was more reliable *(not to mention more favorable)* than his circumstances. Be like Abraham and consider not *(your circumstances, see Romans 4:19,20)* what you may have become.

Remember: Our view is like watching a parade through a pin hole. Take God's word for it. He sees the whole picture.

"The rarest courage is the courage of thought."

Anatole France

You Are (UR) -- framing your world.

SEPTEMBER 10 *(HEBREWS 11:3)*

Your tongue is the most powerful tool you have for shaping the world you live in. Pastor Cho of Korea once expressed it this way. *"I dip the paint brush of my tongue into the palate of God's word and paint the vision on the canvas of my heart."*

You Are (UR) -- free from terror.

SEPTEMBER 11 *(PSALM 91)*

On this date in 2001, the world witnessed the unimagineable. Airplanes, commandeered by terrorists, crashed into the twin towers of The World Trade Center. Americans were under siege on their own soil for the first time since the Civil War *(or the Revolutionary War -- depending on whom you ask).*

Time stood still as the images were replayed again and again creating a compelling backdrop as the pundits and prognosticators pedaled their pontifications from place to place and fear became the coin of the realm.

Markets reeled. Accusations flew. Detention camps reappeared, curiously shiny and new. Homeland Security became a funded fact. And our personal privacy became a part of the act.

On this date in 2001, Matthew 24 became alarmingly relevant. Time disappeared and Jesus' ancient warnings became our immediate reality. The love of many did wax cold. And for many, the waxing has not waned.

David said it best in Psalm 20:6-8. *"Some trust in chariots, and some in horses: but we will remember the name of the LORD our God."* Truly, we are dwelling in the secret place of the most high and we will say of the Lord: He is our refuge, our God in Him will we trust. We are free from terror.

You Are (UR) -- doing well.

On July 27, I wrote that people keep asking me how I'm doing. My answer then was: *"Compared to what?"* My rationale was: *"It's too soon to tell."* I still believe that, but I think I have a better answer now. I have an answer that is better for me and better for them because it better declares the word of God. **Say it out loud!**

"I am doing well."

Because English is such a peculiar language, most will assume that every thing is all right and that my situation is good. Either that or they'll take it as just another piece of social patter to cover the many troubles that we all face from day to day and gladly move on without having to get involved. And, depending on what day it is, either may be true.

What will always be true, however, is that no matter what my situation or circumstances are, I am committed to continue, without weariness, in well doing. And because I know that by doing so I will reap in due season if I faint not, I could even make the declaration of the great Shunamite woman of 2 Kings 4; *"It is well."*

You Are (UR) -- going to have a good day.

Say it out loud! The king's commandment and his decree are gone forth. The enemy who intended to destroy me is himself destroyed. Today I will have joy and gladness, a feast and a good day. I will open my mouth and sing a new song. And many shall see it and fear and put their trust in the Lord. (Psalm 40:1-3) I am going to have a good day.

You Are (UR) -- special.

SEPTEMBER 14 *(1 TIMOTHY 4:9-11)*

God loves everybody and wants no one to perish. (2 Peter 3:9) Jesus died for whosoever and wants all to be saved. (John 3:16) Our father is no respecter of persons, and causes the sun to rise on the evil and the good and the rain to fall on the just and the unjust. (Acts 10:34 / Matthew 5:45) But there is a special place in his heart for them who believe.

The disciples knew it and called John *"the disciple whom Jesus loved."* (John 21:20) Thomas experienced it when he demanded to see and touch the nail prints and thrust his hand into Jesus' side before he would believe. He got what he asked for, but Jesus was emphatic about the preferred place of those who have not seen, and yet have believed.

God treasures believers. He searches them out. He is seeking people who will serve him in *"Spirit and in truth."* (John 4:24) And while the devil is *"walking to and fro"* seeking unbelievers he may devour, *"the eyes of the Lord run to and fro throughout the whole earth, to show himself strong in the behalf of them whose heart is perfect toward him."* (2 Chronicles 16:9) Keep on believing. You are special.

You Are (UR) -- ministers of reconciliation.

SEPTEMBER 15 *(2 COR. 5:14-19)*

We are here to restore relationships. People to God. People to people. One enables the other. The other proves the one. It is God who initiated the cycle. (John 3:16) He so loved us so that we might love him. Now that we love him we ought to love one another. (1 John 3:16) If we don't love others, how can we say we love him? (1 John 4:7-21) Any questions? You are ministers of reconciliation.

You Are (UR) -- in an impossible situation.

(MATT. 14:22-33) SEPTEMBER 16

What you have to do is not only possible, but quite natural. When Peter walked on water to Jesus, he was not doing anything he hadn't done before. All his life, as a fisherman, he had stepped out of that boat and walked. What was different, on this day, was what he was walking on. God will never ask you to do anything you can't do. Even if you've never done it before, the fact that He asks you to do it establishes its possibility.

Now, He may very well ask you to do things in seemingly impossible situations and under unbelievable conditions. And all of us who know Him, are well aware that He tends to ask at the worst possible time *(generally the last minute)*. But that is where one must walk by faith, eyes firmly focused on Jesus, looking not at the things which are seen. One must do what comes natural in the most unnatural of surroundings. For with God nothing shall be impossible. (Luke 1:37)

You Are (UR) -- sin repellent.

(JOHN 21:23) SEPTEMBER 17

You possess the power to neutralize Satan's effect in the earth. (Luke 10:19 / Matthew 16:18 / 2 Thessalonians 2:7) Your love hides a multitude of sin. (James 5:19,20) The power of the gospel in your mouth delivers the multitudes from their sin. And you are dead to sin. (Romans 6:1,2)

Note: Should sin get the best of you, your lawyer -- your advocate -- Jesus died and rose again for your sins, and his father promises to forgive your sins and cleanse you from all unrighteousness if you will just confess. (1 John 1:9 / 1 John 2:1,2)

You Are (UR) -- working out.

SEPTEMBER 18 *(PHIL. 2:12,13)*

It's nice to know that people are satisfied with your performance. Especially when they are people in authority and have some say-so about how you continue. That pat on the back or a timely thumbs up can make all the difference. But always remember: *"...promotion cometh neither from the east, nor from the west, nor from the south. But God is the judge: he putteth down one, and setteth up another."* (Psalm 75:6,7)

At the end of the day, You want to hear God say, *"Well done thou good and faithful servant."* In order to get that performance appraisal right, you are going to have to work out. You are going to have to *"work out your own salvation with fear and trembling. For it is God which worketh in you both to will and to do of his good pleasure."*

You Are (UR) -- seeking the kingdom.

SEPTEMBER 19 *(MATTHEW 6:33)*

When Mickey Mouse made his debut on this day in 1928, I'm not sure even Walt Disney knew his animated mouse was seeking a "Magic Kingdom." Walter Elias Disney did grow up around kingdom-seeking parents -- in an age of kingdom builders. He was named after his parents' pastor, "Walter Parr," and spent his first five years on earth under the vicarious vision of John Alexander Dowie, founder of the Christian Catholic Church and establisher of Zion, Illinois.

Though I doubt they ever met, Disney built both his theme parks using Dowie's ideas and ideals. Both men disguised themselves and bought cheap land from farmers to establish "better cities." We seek a city also, *"whose builder and maker is God."* (Hebrews 11:8,9) Mickey was a second chance for Walt. His first mouse, Mortimer, was stolen. But Walt didn't quit, and neither will you. Jesus is your second chance. And you, too, are seeking a kingdom. You are seeking the kingdom of God.

You Are (UR) -- waiting patiently.

(PSALM 27:14) SEPTEMBER 20

It's becoming clearer and clearer, day by day, that this is a waiting game. No matter who you are, where you are, what you have accomplished, acquired or achieved -- there are areas in your life where you are waiting on the Lord. You are waiting in a time continuum that demands persistence, patience and unwavering faith. You are also waiting in a servant's posture, attending to that which concerns your master with unflinching focus. You are waiting patiently on the Lord. You wait because He is worth waiting for. *"To whom shall we go?"* Peter responded when asked if he would leave Jesus. To whom indeed? We will wait on the Lord. *"Wait on the Lord: be of good courage, and he shall strengthen thine heart:"* David said. *"Wait, I say, on the Lord."*

You Are (UR) -- singing a new song.

(PSALM 40:1-3) SEPTEMBER 21

People hear songs on the radio and tap their feet to the beat. They hum the tune and mangle the words 'til they get to the part they know. But the song in your heart is no sing-along. Yours is the song of the Lord. Spirits feel your song. They will see it and fear and put their trust in him. What kind of song is this new song? What is this song of the Lord? The song you're singing is a song of praise that worships the most high God. It resonates from deep in your soul and resounds from heaven to hell. The song you're singing overwhelms the ear, the taste, the touch, the smell. The song you are singing is a gift from God. Yours is the song of the Lord. The song you are singing is a gift to God. You are singing a brand new song.

"What is it then? I will pray with the spirit, and I will pray with the understanding also: I will sing with the spirit, and I will sing with the understanding also." (1 Corinthians 14:15)

You Are (UR) -- Christ's prisoner.

SEPTEMBER 22 *(EPESHIANS 3:1)*

The calling on your life may not be quite as dramatic and grandiose as Paul's, but you are yet Christ's captive. He has caught you. And like Paul, you must endeavor to catch what he caught you for.

While preaching a tent revival in Bristitsa, Romania, many years ago, I asked if I could speak in one of the local churches on Sunday. A gracious pastor invited me to speak and I went with a translator to the service. We met in front of their brand-new sanctuary. *(Ceucescu, the recently slain dictator, had bulldozed the old one a year earlier with thirty people in it.)*

Not knowing the language, I inquired about simple ways to greet the people. *"How do you say, Praise the Lord,"* I asked. I was surprised to find that this was not a common saying in the church. Confused, I persisted; *"So how do you express your love for God?"* The pastor humbly replied: *"We say Slava Domnilui."* The translator smiled as she boldly proclaimed, *"Slaves to Jesus."*

You Are (UR) -- running out of time.

SEPTEMBER 23 *(ROMANS 13:11,12)*

Each new day brings us closer to the return of Jesus. And though I know it's not true, the days seem to be moving faster. Our instructions are clear: Wake up! Look around! Straighten up! And get your priorities straight! (Ephesians 5:14-17) We are running out of time and the devil is, too. The devil knows his days are numbered and he's not happy about it. (Revelation 12:9-12) His dismay comes from an awareness that many Christians don't seem to possess. He knows we are all running out of time -- into eternity. *"Look up, and lift up your heads; for your redemption draweth nigh."* (Luke 21:28) Now is a good time to tell somebody. We are running out of time.

You Are (UR) -- about your Father's business.

People are looking for you. They are wondering where you are. They miss you at the club. They thought you had a date. Your opinion is needed at the table of discussion. You may feel a little out of place. You may even feel pressured to return. But never forget: You are about your Father's business.

Life has changed. Actually, life has just begun. You are a new creature in Christ Jesus. *"Old things are passed away."* Will you see the old crew again? Probably. Jesus went home with his parents on that ominous day that foretold his true purpose. He went home with them physically and geographically, but his spirit and soul had already begun their journey into the things of God. And just like Mary and Joseph, people may question, but in their hearts they know: You are about your Father's business.

You Are (UR) -- being used.

Only in America could a thing so wonderful as being used be confused with being abused. News flash! If you are being used, it means you are useful. Now, if you feel you are overly taxed or even being mistreated, learn to say no. Say it and mean it. But learn to say it with a smile on your face and the joy of the Lord in your heart. (Romans 12:1-8)

And make it clear that you are saying no to a specific task or situation rather than the thought of being called upon. Because as weary as you feel now from being used, the hardest work you will ever do is trying to get used once you've lost your usefulness. **Say it out loud!** I am being used.

You Are (UR) -- a beloved child in whom God is well pleased.

SEPTEMBER 26 *(MATT. 3:13-17)*

There are men and women all over the world who have waited their whole lives to hear a mom or dad express loving pleasure in them. We know our parents love us just as we believe that God loves us. But do they like us? Are they pleased with us? Are they happy with and/or proud of what we are becoming or have become?

Unfortunately, natural parents, unlike God, are neither omniscient nor omnipotent. They cannot see the end from the beginning any better than we can. They must walk by faith or merely declare what they see. God is well pleased with you because He made you and He knows that having begun a good work in you, He will also perform it until the day of Jesus Christ. (Philippians 1:6)

Lt. Col. David Kithcart once told me that my life is like a movie that God has already seen. That is why He could love Jacob and hate Esau. In His sovereignty He has chosen to give us *(yes, Esau too)* a choice. We can choose to believe that we are made in His image and likeness and that He is pleased with what He made. Or we can be deceived, like Eve, into believing that this is all a trick and God is out to get us. That faith -- one way or the other -- will govern our choices and determine our outcomes. So I say again. You are a beloved child in whom God is well pleased.

You Are (UR) -- making the most of today.

SEPTEMBER 27 *(MATT. 6:25-34)*

"No matter what looms ahead, if you can eat today, enjoy the sunlight today, mix good cheer with friends today, enjoy it and bless God for it. Do not look back on happiness -- or dream of it in the future. You are only sure of today: do not let yourself be cheated out of it." Henry Ward Beecher *(father of Harriet Beecher Stowe - author of Uncle Tom's Cabin)*

You Are (UR) -- the sheep of His hand.

(Psalm 23) **September 28**

Maybe you should sit down -- no -- lie down. Isn't it strange that God has to make us lie down? And that in green pastures. That notwithstanding, even in these green pastures we are often so distraught with worry and anxiety that we can't even see good when it comes. (Jeremiah 17:5,6)

God says, *"Lie down!"* He shuts us up like Zacharias. (Luke 1:19,20) He hedges us in like Balaam. (Numbers 22:22-26) He makes us taste and see that the Lord is good. Why? Because He knows our frame. He remembers that we are dust. (Psalm 103:14) He knows what He made us from and that we need His mercy to survive. He knows we need His pity and His grace to thrive. He is our shepherd and we are the sheep of his hand.

You Are (UR) -- before Abraham.

(John 8:58) **September 29**

This series of daily encouraging words began with a simple idea. Jesus claimed that any man who kept his saying would never taste of death. The Pharisees challenged him using Abraham and the prophets as a measure. Jesus tried to convince them that He was not a liar and assured them that even Abraham *"rejoiced"* to see His day. This really infuriated them so they hit him with the thing that limited them most -- time.

"Thou art not yet fifty years old," they said; *"hast thou seen Abraham?"* Jesus never missed a beat and neither should you. **Say it out loud!** Before (Abraham, Sickness, Debt, Divorce, Death, Addiction, Lay Off, Sin, etc..., etc..., ad infinitum) was -- I am. I am saved, healed, filled with the Holy Ghost, forgiven, a witness, called, chosen, faithful, a saint, the righteousness of God in Christ Jesus, etc..., etc..., ad in Jesus. God is. And I am -- everything he says I am. I transcend circumstance and outlive time. I am before Abraham.

You Are (UR) -- runnin' and ain't nothin' at ya.

SEPTEMBER 30 *(PROVERBS 28:1)*

For those of you who didn't have a good grandma like mine (smile), that is translated: *"You are running and there is nothing after you."* The devil is defeated. Jesus is Lord. You are forgiven. And all things are yours. This fearful, anxious, condemnation thing you've got going must be confusing -- to you, the devil, the angels and to God. Even King David asked himself, *"Why art thou cast down O my soul? and why art thou disquieted within me?"* (Psalm 43:5)

God wants to know the same thing. He asks, *"I, even I, am he that comforteth you: who art thou, that thou shouldst be afraid of a man that shall die, and of the son of man which shall be made as grass; And forgettest the Lord thy maker, that hath stretched forth the heavens, and laid the foundations of the earth: and hast feared continually every day because of the fury of the oppressor, as if he were ready to destroy? And where is the fury of the oppressor?"* (Isaiah 51:12,13)

I love God's righteous indignation. *"As if...,"* he says. *"And where is..."* the devil anyhow? I'll tell you where he is. The devil is walking to and fro, *"as a roaring lion,"* looking for righteous people who should be *"bold as a lion,"* to give him permission to destroy their lives.

Well, David got it right and you will, too. He answered his own question with these bold words. **Say it out loud!** *"Hope in God: for I shall yet praise him, who is the health of my countenance and my God."* Be like David and hope in God; otherwise you'll find yourself runnin' and ain't nothin' at ya.

---

*"Success is never final and Failure never fatal.
It is courage that counts."*

George F. Tilton

You Are (UR) -- naked.

We've all had the dream. You know, the one where you are stark naked in a crowd of people. Some of us run. Some cover the "critical" parts. Others are frozen with fear like a deer before headlights. Whatever the reaction, we are all ashamed. We are ashamed of our insufficiency, our unpreparedness and our vulnerability. We are ashamed like Adam and Eve were when they sinned against God. But wait! God put them in the garden naked. And prior to their sin, they were naked and unashamed. (Genesis 2:25)

When God chastened them, he never denied their nakedness. He simply asked, *"Who told you that you were naked?"* It's a good question. After all, what does it matter and why are we so focused on it? (Matthew 6:23-34) Everybody came here naked and naked is how everyone will leave. (1 Timothy 6:7) And no matter what their covering in the interim, everyone feels a bit underclad from time to time. It's why so many people are looking for MORE. They are trying to cover their buts. (Not a typo;-) *"I would like to be, do, or have a, b, or c: BUT, I don't have e, f, or g."*

What you need is some AND to cover your BUT. Jabez's mother called him Jabez because she bore him with sorrow AND he was more honorable than his brethren. (1 Chronicles 4:9,10) You're naked AND God has you covered. So the next time someone points out your nakedness *(Well, you don't have this. Or, you don't know that.)*, just look at him incredulously and ask, *"AND?"* You will find that you are very well covered.

"Courage is resistance to fear, mastery of fear -- not absence of fear. Except a creature be part coward, it is not a compliment to say it is brave; it is merely a loose misapplication of the word."

Mark Twain

You Are (UR) -- not dropping the ball.

OCTOBER 2 *(ROMANS 13:11,12))*

When experienced fielders began dropping fly balls that any little leaguer should catch, area sports writers asked why. In an attempt to explain the distracting movement of pre Daylight Savings Time shadows in Yankee Stadium's outfield, legendary manager Yogi Berra responded in classic fashion. He said, *"It gets late early."* Hey! When God is moving, the shadows do funky things. And it is getting *"late early."* But Jesus is Daylight Savings Time. (Joel 2:25)

You Are (UR) -- not guilty.

OCTOBER 3 *(ROMANS 4:1-8)*

The headlines indicate that there is some real confusion about our relative guilt or innocence. *"He Was An Innocent Bystander." "OJ Did It!" "Ossama Bin Laden - The Face of Evil." "6000 Innocent Victims Slain In Terror Attacks."* Unless I have misread the scriptures, nobody's innocent. All have sinned and come short of the glory of God. (Romans 3:23) Our only comfort is that Jesus bore our sins in his own body on the tree being made sin for us. (2 Peter 2:24) While we were yet sinners, Christ died for the ungodly. (Romans 5:8) We who have received him have been justified -- made right -- redeemed by the blood of the Lamb.

Did OJ kill Nicole? All I know is, he was declared *"not guilty,"* by a jury of his peers. I wasn't there and neither was Cedric the Entertainer. But whether he did or not, the fact that he was sold into sin by Adam made him worthy of death and hell. And neither we nor Cedric nor any one of the thousands killed in 9/11, including their attackers, deserves any better. But thank God, all believers have been declared, *"NOT GUILTY!"* *"Not by works of righteousness which we have done, but according to his mercy, he saved us by the washing of regeneration and renewing of the Holy Ghost."* (Titus 3:3-5) **Say it out loud!** I am not guilty!

You Are (UR) -- out of focus.

(MARK 8:22-25) OCTOBER 4

There is something about change that causes blindness. And failure or success doesn't seem to matter. The fact that you are not where people left you -- the truth that you are not what was expected, can blur even your vision of yourself.

Strange that the human mind cannot balance two differing images of one thing when its creator does this so well. True, *"No man can serve two masters."* (Matthew 6:22-24) And perhaps that is why we find this delicate balance so difficult to preserve. We tend to serve the images we hold, rather than the God who imagined us in the first place.

God sees you in two, becoming one. He sees the you that He imagined and the you that you have become and calls the you that is not as though you were. (Romans 4:13-17) He sent Jesus to reconcile the images. In the mean time, unless you accept his view of you, you are out of focus.

You Are (UR) -- changing.

(2 CORINTHIANS 3:18) OCTOBER 5

Mirror, mirror on the wall. Who's the fairest of them all? The answer, of course, is Snow White, unless your mirror is the perfect law of liberty. Then, Jesus, "The fairest of ten thousand" as the songwriter calls him, makes our sins which were as scarlet, white as snow. (Isaiah 1:17-19)

Suddenly, we who are changed into the image of Christ, *"from glory to glory,"* are looking much better. Now don't go off and forget what you look like. Be a doer of the work and be blessed in your deeds. (James 1:22-25)

You Are (UR) -- a prayer making, prison breaker.

OCTOBER 6 *(ACTS 12:1-16)*

Peter was a political prisoner. He was locked up purely because Herod saw that the execution of James pleased the Jews. Much of what is happening to righteous brethren around the world is also attack by association. (Hebrews 10:32-39) It is those same associations, however, that will be their (your) deliverance.

The saints made prayer "without ceasing." The angels responded to that prayer -- ministering for them. (Hebrews 1:14) The prison was shaken and Peter was led to safety. Could others' "way of escape" be dependent on our prayers? (1 Corinthians 10:13) **Say it out loud!** YES! We are prayer making, prison breakers.

You Are (UR) -- going to find what you are looking for.

OCTOBER 7 *(LUKE 11:5-13)*

God is not hiding. He is actually looking for people who are looking for Him. (John 4:20-24 / 2 Chronicles 16:9) As illusive as He may seem and as distant as His voice may sound, it is really a matter of sincere interest, persistence and time. When you want to find Him and won't take no for an answer, He will be right where He has always been: *"a very present help in time of trouble."* (Psalm 46:1)

"Call me," He says. (Psalm 50:15) *"Ask and it shall be given you, seek, and ye shall find, knock, and it shall be opened unto you."* These are God's words to you and me. He means them and He has the means to back them up. Settle in: you will find it very rewarding, indeed, to seek diligently after Him. He Is...what you are looking for. (Hebrews 11:6)

You Are (UR) -- somebody.

(ROMANS 12:6-8) OCTOBER 8

On October 8, 1941, one of the world's great encouragers was born. It was Jesse L. Jackson, Sr. who told us years ago that we were somebody. Many of us may still be trying to figure out who we are, but for a lot of us, it was the Rev. Jackson who encouraged the march toward self discovery. Here is an excerpt from the March on the Capital: Monday, October 27, 1997 - Sacramento, California, declaring the power of the march.

"When we march, we affirm our resolve to dignity. When we march, we exercise one of our great freedoms, the right to protest for the right. When we march, we motivate. We educate. We expand the public debate. We alter the environment. When we march, we inspire. We raise hope to new levels. When we march together in coalition, with determination, driven by the moral imperative, we almost always win. Marching is always in contrast to surrendering, cynicism, loss of confidence and doing nothing. Dr. King warned that we had to move beyond a paralysis of analysis, to direct action.

We march in a great tradition. When Moses marched across the Red Sea, the moral imperative could not be ignored. It altered the course of human history. The marchers changed public policy. When Joshua marched around the walls, steadfastly and with determination, seven days and seven nights, nobody could get in and nobody could get out. It was a boycott. The walls of division and oppression came tumbling down.

When Jesus marched with a rugged cross of redemption and reconciliation and selfless suffering, it had healing power. When Gandhi marched to the sea, it led to the freedom of a great, but beleaguered nation. When Dr. King marched in Washington projecting the dream, and marched across the Edmund Pettus bridge in Selma for the right to vote, with the willingness to die so that others might live, those marches generated hope and strength and a renewal of faith.

There is power in our marching feet. Today, Dr. King would say we face the fierce urgency of now. We cannot wait and we cannot go backwards now, for the time to coalesce and build an ark is as the flood waters rise. We will survive the flood. We can get better and not bitter. If we are determined and not distracted, we will save the dream, and sustain hope.

And so we march until mountains are made low and until valleys are exalted. Until crooked ways are made straight. Until the least of these have their right to the tree of life. We march for all of us to say with assurance that this land is our land. It was made for you and me. We will march until the song of hope resounds from every valley and mountainside. In many languages there will be a common message that says, yes we can!"

Thank you Rev. Jackson for reminding me that I am somebody.

You Are (UR) -- made in God's image.

OCTOBER 9 *(GENESIS 1:26,27)*

You are made in God's image. But are you what he imagined? I'll speak for myself and assure you that I am not. At least -- not yet. There is a process taking place that even Adam experienced. Adam became a living soul when God's spirit was blown into that which was formed. Then through disobedience, Adam became something other than what God imagined.

We are instructed to cast down imaginations and every high thing that exalteth itself against the knowledge of God. (2 Corinthians 10:5) Is it possible that God may be doing the same thing? Could our Father, in whose image we are made, be battling the thought of us becoming anything other than that which He imagined? Imagine this. God is not a quitter. He is a finisher. (Hebrews 12:1,2) He didn't give up on Adam and He won't give up on you. You are made in God's image. And if you can agree with He says, you will be what He sees.

You Are (UR) -- not God.

OCTOBER 10 *(JOB 38)*

Or as a dear friend can say so well: *"Ain't nobody God but God."* What a relief. I lay hands. He heals the sick. (Mark 16:15-18) I submit myself to Him. Devils flee. (James 4:7) I seek His kingdom. He rewards me and meets my needs. (Matthew 6:33 / Hebrews 11:6) I repent. He forgives and cleanses. (1 John 1:9)

It's a sweet arrangement. And lest you forget: The last time someone tried to replace God, all hell broke loose -- literally. (Isaiah 14:9-17) **Say it out loud!** *"Ain't nobody God but God."*

You Are (UR) -- being talked about.

(ACTS 11:26) OCTOBER 11

When you act like Jesus *(preaching the gospel, laying hands on sick people, casting out devils, etc...)*, it stirs conversation. People will label your behavior and it may surprise you what they say. Jesus understood this when he asked the disciples, *"whom do men say that I, the Son of man, am?"* (Matthew 16:13-18) People called him John the Baptist, Elijah, Jeremiah, and God knows what else. The Pharisees even called him a demon-possessed Samaritan. (John 8:48) I have been called holier than thou, judgmental, intolerant, goody two shoes, a Bible-thumper, crazy and a few things I won't repeat. Since no one likes to be disliked or misunderstood, it is important to understand these misnomers.

The prophets and John the Baptist were the last people anyone remembered acting the way Jesus did. The Pharisees were embarrassed that their supposed relationship with God did not produce the results that Jesus' did. And Christ was the most recent example that could be compared to the Antioch disciples' behavior. As time passes and the world becomes less familiar with the scriptures they are going to look for ways to describe Christ like behavior. Stick to the book and do all in the name of Jesus, giving him the glory, and be glad: you are being talked about.

You Are (UR) -- getting a second chance.

(MATTHEW 18:23-35) OCTOBER 12

Say it out loud! Thank you Lord for forgiving me. I know I owed a debt that I could not pay. Please help me to remember that your grace demands my graciousness. Let me never forget that your mercy must produce mercy in me. Everything that I am, everything that I have, everthing that I ever hope to be is an unspeakable gift from you. I am thankful Lord and I stand amazed that you love me. I purpose in my heart to live a life of forgiveness, and to use this chance to give others a chance to change.

You Are (UR) -- in need of patience.

OCTOBER 13 *(HEBREWS 10:35-39)*

You have done the will of God. You have repented. You are saved. You will not perish because you have come to the knowledge of the truth. (1 Timothy 2:1-4 / 2 Peter 3:9) There are great and precious promises established for you that you might take your part of the divine nature. You have escaped the corruption that is in the world. (2 Peter 1:1-4)

Don't quit. Don't give up. Don't faint. Don't grow weary in well doing. You shall reap. (Galatians 6:7-9) Your season is coming. It must, because the earth remains. (Genesis 8:22) Now is not the time to murmur and complain. Now is the time to rejoice. You will be tried, tempted, tested, and tricked. Count it all joy. Patience is being worked in you and that is exactly what you need. Soon and very soon, you will be perfect and entire, wanting nothing. (James 1:1-5)

You Are (UR) -- outnumbered.

OCTOBER 14 *(1 JOHN 3:19-21)*

Surrender! You can't win. Give up! There is no escape. You are outnumbered and outgunned. The blessings and benefits of God are more than you can imagine and more than you can deny. (Ephesians 3:20) You cannot curse what God has blessed. And God has blessed you. (Numbers 22:12) Why fight? Why struggle? Why even consider the trouble before you? (Romans 4:16-21) What you currently suffer is not worthy to be compared with the glory that shall be revealed in you. (Romans 8:18) Patience is waiting -- waiting to go to work on your behalf. Patience is waiting to manage the temps (temporary troubles) at your disposal. (James 1:1-4) So rest, and let them work together for your good. (Romans 8:28) Rest, and soon you will be perfect and entire -- wanting nothing. There is no need to resist any longer. You are outnumbered.

You Are (UR) -- in labor.

(Ecclesiastes 1:8) OCTOBER 15

Actually, labor is in you. You are full of it. And it is full of profit. (Proverbs 14:23) You do the math. If you are full of labor and in all labor there is profit, then you are full of profit. So why don't you see it? Well, it has to be born of the Spirit. (John 3:6) And all of creation awaits your delivery, because *"...the manifestation of the Spirit is given to every man to profit withal."* (Romans 8:18,19 / 1 Corinthians 12:7 / 1 Timothy 4:14-16)

You Are (UR) -- facing a deadline.

(2 Corinthians 3) OCTOBER 16

Ahhhh! The point of no return. The end of the line. The end of your rope. The last minute, drop dead date. Deadlines. People are always facing them. And people are always crossing them. Why? Because that's what they are -- Dead Lines. The great woman of 2 Kings 4 faced one. Jairus faced one in Mark 5. Mary, Martha and Lazarus faced one in John 11. And you are going to face some, too. So what will you do?

Well, you might do like a woman I know whose son was born one day after the state school deadline. But when she looked at the child, she saw something, much as Moses' mother saw, that no legislator could foresee. So with the stroke of a pen, the child's birthday went from 10/17 to 10/14 and he went to school one year early rather than one year late. She crossed a dead line. Twelve years later, he graduated with honors.

> *"It is strange that men should look back on history and choose as their heroes those who defied their times while at the same instant yield themselves complacently as slaves to their own times and crucify those who live in the future..."*
>
> **William Stuart Nelson**
> The Journal of Religious Thought: **1945**

Whatever you do, you will begin by saying, *"It is well."* You will *"Be not afraid and only believe."* You will defy the dead letter of the coroner's certificate and the smell of decay all around you. And you will *"Come forth!"* You are facing a deadline.

You Are (UR) -- what you are AND what God says you are.

OCTOBER 17 *(1 CHRONICLES 4:9,10)*

AND spelled backwards is DNA. An odd coincidence when you consider that the world is obsessed with this powerful string of genetic gobble-dygook. From stem cells to cloning to solving the world's problems with a procedure or a pill, the gene pool is swimming with "possibilities." Or is it?

Jabez didn't seem to think so. Sure, his mother named him Jabez because she bore him with sorrow, but he didn't buy into the Freudian theory of life blamed on mother and he didn't take a dive into the DNA deep either. No he flipped the genes on their head and took an end run around mother, straight to Father.

Say it out loud! *"AND Jabez called on God."* I don't know what your family tree looks like, but if it's like mine, it's got a few bad apples, hanging on some shaky limbs and the worms are at work from the root to the fruit. AND you are still all the things God said you were from before the foundation of the world.

You Are (UR) -- why.

OCTOBER 18 *(AMOS 4:6-11)*

Everybody wants to know why. Why am I going through this? Why did that happen to me? Why didn't I get the job? Why don't I have a spouse?

Why? Why? Why? Why? Why?

The answer is simple. You are why. No matter what you are going through, God is after you. Now that I have your attention, God has a question. *"Why won't you turn to me?"*

You Are (UR) -- in over your head.

The children of Israel walked into the miracle God had made. Instantly, millions of them, young and old, were in over their heads. Sure, they were walking on dry land. But just the night before, that virgin path had been the bottom of the deep Red Sea. And every step of their marvelous move, they were surrounded by walls of living water. Talk about jumping into the deep end.

The attitude of the day had to be trust. Trust Moses. Trust God. Trust that the good thing that is now happening is truer than the opposing tradition *(currently crashing like breakers against the walls of your mind)* that you once trusted. All we who trust in the living God are in over our heads. He is leading us through the depths of the impossible to the safety of his glorious grace.

You Are (UR) -- in over your head.

Have you ever been around people who you thought were extraordinary? In minutes you become terrified, by comparison, that you don't have a shot, you can't win the game, and you are outmanned and outgunned in the deal. In short, you are in over your head. That's the feeling that fills the room every time Jesus enters. (Luke 5:8)

David articulated it better than most. *"What is man, that thou art mindful of him?"* he asked, in Psalm 8. In that case, he was just marveling at the things God had made. It can be humiliating to believe that you really don't belong. And then the Lord of the house opens His arms and receives you without condemnation -- filling you with all His fulness. (Ephesians 3:14-19) Then and only then are you glad to be in over your head.

You Are (UR) -- in over your head.

OCTOBER 21 *(JONAH 2:1-9)*

Pressure always pushes to preference. In other words, when the going gets tough, people tend to go where they really wanted to anyhow. And believe it or not, they don't always want to go toward the Lord. (See Amos 4:6-11) Jonah is the Bible's classic example. But Jonah ultimately redeemed himself under pressure.

Yes, Jonah ran from God's command. Yes, Jonah went down to Joppa. Yes, he went down into the boat. But it wasn't God he was trying to avoid. It was the people of Nineveh. And when he realized that there was no changing God's mind, he repented and cried out to God -- the God of his salvation.

So before you condemn Jonah, remember, Jesus was not in any hurry to go to the cross either. Gethsemane is down the hill from Calvary. And both men cracked under pressure. They both were pushed to broken hearts and contrite spirits. They both realized they were in over their heads.

You Are (UR) -- in over your head.

OCTOBER 22 *(2 CHRONICLES 20:12)*

King Jeshoshaphat knew he was in beyond his depth. Like any normal human being, he feared when he heard he was being attacked. But it was what he did when he feared that determined his destiny. He set himself to seek the Lord. *"Seek ye first...."* How could Jeshoshaphat have known this principal of Jesus? (Matthew 6:33) He called a fast and prayed.

True to His word, God answered and delivered. And all of Israel glorified him. Miracles are generally born out of messes. King Jeshoshaphat fell down to worship and stood up to praise because he was first willing to admit that he was in over his head.

You Are (UR) -- in over your head.

(GENESIS 6 & 7) OCTOBER 23

Noah lived in a world *"filled with violence"* and God was about to destroy and displace the violent with water. Noah was definitely in over his head. But where sin abounds, grace doth much more abound. And *"Noah found grace in the eyes of the Lord."*

It is unclear how many years it took Noah to build the ark and load it to God's specifications. It is unmistakeable, however, that he was surrounded by things bigger than himself. Lions and tigers and bears -- oh and elephants. And one must not forget a world of angry sinners who mocked him day and night as he warned them of the wrath to come.

As the ark began to tower into the heavens, Noah must have been keenly aware of his comparative insignificance. Only one thing kept him afloat -- the knowledge of God. That was the most important thing that boarded that ark. That and that alone held back the waters. For all practical purposes, the ark was a submarine. The waters came from above and beneath. But humanity continues because Noah and his family got in over their heads.

You Are (UR) -- granted your request.

(1 CHRONICLES 4:9,10) OCTOBER 24

There is no magic lamp. No genies will be appearing. And your seemingly insurmountable obstacle is common to all people. It is the face of such difficulty that you might one day turn to God. (Acts 17:24-27) The answer is the same for you as it was for all who came before you: Adam, Cain, Noah, Abraham, Rahab, Ruth, Joseph, Gideon, Hezekiah, Esther, Jonah, Jephthah, Jabez, David, Peter, and even Jesus. *"Yes."* (2 Corinthians 1:19,20) *"Yes. You are called. Yes. You are chosen. Yes. You are forgiven. Yes. You shall live. Yes. I will sustain you. Yes. There is more. Yes. I can still use you. Yes! Yes! Yes! Yes! Yes! You are granted your request."*

You Are (UR) -- abiding under the shadow of the Almighty.

OCTOBER 25 *(PSALM 91)*

Quick! Think like a kid and make a shadow on the nearest wall. Now! Think like an adult and consider how it's made. There is something between the light and the shadow. Still thinking? Consider this.

> *"Every good gift and every perfect gift is from above,*
> *and cometh down from the Father of lights,*
> *with whom is no variableness, neither shadow of turning."*
> James 1:17

Rough translation -- God is at peak performance, like the noonday sun above a sun dial, over all who trust in Him, at all times. He never changes and therefore -- casts no shadow. So where is this *"shadow of the Almighty"?* In Him!

We are dwelling in the secret place of the Most High. Our life is hid with Christ -- in God. What's between the light and the shadow we dwell under? All the fulness of God himself. You are abiding under the shadow of the Almighty.

You Are (UR) -- content.

OCTOBER 26 *(PHILIPPIANS 4:10-13)*

Aren't you? Yes. You are. Sure -- you're on the move, trying to catch the dream that Jesus caught you for. (Philippians 3:12) You may be going through a tough spot in the process. *(Operative words being -- going through)* Or perhaps you are enjoying some good fortune, and worry that even that can be fleeting. Just never forget who got you there. (Proverbs 30:7-9) And remember, no matter where you find yourself, you can say *"It is well,"* (2 Kings 4:18-26) because God is with you. He promised He will never leave you or forsake you. And wherever He is taking you is far better than where you were going before you decided to go with Him.

You Are (UR) -- eligible for Witness Protection.

(PROVERBS 14:25) OCTOBER 27

The devil is out to silence you. (1 Peter 5:8/John 10:10) He knows that your testimony will set captives free and hinder his ability to wreak havoc on the earth. (Revelation 12:10-12) Have you considered Witness Protection? Jesus wants to expunge your past, (Philippians 3:13) give you a new vocation, (Ephesians 4:1-4) and change your name, appearance, and nature, so that you can be a witness for Him. (1 Samuel 10:1-6/2 Corinthians 5:17)

You Are (UR) -- the spitting image of your Father.

(HEBREWS 1:1-4) OCTOBER 28

I have spent my entire life trying to be an individual. I wanted my own personal style. I moved out of my father's house and set out to make it on my own. But try as I may, the older I get, the more I look like him.

All relationships go through their own peculiar adolescence -- even our relationship with God. (1 John 2:12-14) We all have to *"overcome the wicked one"* -- the beast full of 'I's' (Isaiah 14:9-17 esp. vss. 13 & 14) that wants to separate us from our Father. But beware the strength of the blood.

The blood of Christ on you and the Spirit and the Word of God in you, are changing you. Accessorize and individualize all you want. One day you are going to just disappear (Hebrews 11:5) and people are going to see less of you and more of Him.

"Every man of courage is a man of his word."

Pierre Corneille

You Are (UR) -- getting hungry.

OCTOBER 29 *(2 THESS. 3:6-10)*

The mandate is moving. The message is clear. *"If any would not work, neither should he eat."* I love to eat. I can say, without hesitation, it is one of my favorite things. *"Blessed are they which are called unto the marriage supper of the Lamb."* (Revelation 19:6-9) Amen! But dinner is after work. We eat when the work is finished.

When the disciples returned to Sychar of Samaria after finding food, they found the Lord talking to the woman at the well. Surprised at the interaction, the disciples waited until she left and then begged him to eat. *"I have meat to eat that you know not of,"* He said. Seeing their confusion, he continued, *"My meat is to do the will of Him that sent me and to finish His work."* (John 4:27-34) And finish, He did.

Jesus finished because He was hungry. He hungered and thirsted after righteousness. (Matthew 5:6) No amount of wishing, hoping, or even begging would satisfy that hunger. He knew He would eat the labour of his hands (Psalm 128:2) -- His hands, His feet, His back, His heart. Jesus was a doer of the work and He was blessed in His deed. (James 1:22-25) He was hungry and knew *"that if any would not work neither should he eat."* It's time you went to work, because you are getting hungry.

You Are (UR) -- profitable.

OCTOBER 30 *(PROVERBS 14:23)*

According to Mr. Webster, you yield advantageous returns and results. Your boss knows it. (Read the story of Jacob and Laban: Genesis 28/29/ 30 & 31 especially 30:27) Your friends and enemies know it. (Acts 15:36-42/2 Timothy 4:9-11) And as soon as you believe it *(agree with it - confess it - adjust to it - trust it - rely on it - act on it)*, the Lord will confirm it. Matthew 25:14-30.

You Are (UR) -- the undead.

(John 11:25,26) OCTOBER 31

The ghouls and the ghosts will be at your door this evening, tricked into wanting a treat. Give them a tract with their truffles so that they know they don't have to go where the goblins do. Vampires and zombies are just satanic copies anyhow. They are spiritual wannabes.

You are the true undead. For when we were dead in trespasses and sins, Christ died for the ungodly. Now *"the love of Christ constraineth us; because we thus judge, that if one died for all, then were all dead: And that he died for all, that they which live should not henceforth live unto themselves, but unto him which died for them, and rose again."* (2 Corinthians 5:14,15) You are the undead.

You Are (UR) -- all saints.

(Revelation 8:3) NOVEMBER 1

November 1 has been established as All Saints Day and in Mexico the dead are honored. Generally in the Roman Catholic Church the title *"saint"* is limited to the canonized if they lived after the year 1000; otherwise the title is used according to custom. In East and West criteria for recognition of sainthood are *martyrdom, holiness of life, miracles in life and after death (e.g., with relics), and a popular cultus.*

The addition of the name of a person to the official list of saints occurs through the process of canonization. The Virgin Mary is the chief saint, and the angels are counted as saints. In 1969 the Roman Catholic Church dropped a number of saints from its liturgical calendar because of doubt that they ever lived; among them was the popular St. Christopher. But search your concordance between what God has said and what He now saith and you will find that your name is still on His list -- or in His book I should say. Because we who name the name of Christ are all saints.

You Are (UR) -- God's elect.

NOVEMBER 2 *(ROMANS 8:31-34)*

Today is election day. On the Tuesday on or after this date, US citizens will choose leaders to represent them. And voting is a fundamental right that all members of a democracy should exercise, though confidence in governments has long been on the decline.

While others are limited to a single vote on a given day, however, we as God's elect are granted the privilege of influencing our leaders everyday -- through prayer. (1 Timothy 2:1-4)

God votes too. He is for us. He has chosen us. (John 15:16) He has great expectation for us. (Jeremiah 29:11) So let us -- God's elect -- elect him Lord of our lives each day.

You Are (UR) -- partaking of the divine nature.

NOVEMBER 3 *(2 PETER 1:1-4)*

You have faith -- the God kind of faith. (Hebrews 11:1 / 2 Thessalonians 3:1,2) "Things" that you wouldn't normally talk to, now listen and obey. (Luke 17:6 / Mark 4:35-41) Grace and peace are multiplied to you, so you're enjoying things you don't deserve and worrying less than ever. (Philippians 4:6-8 / Proverbs 10:22) As a matter of fact, you have access to everything you need naturally and spiritually, and God is calling you to walk in his fulness and his power. (John 15:16)

He has made you some promises -- some exceeding great and precious promises. And because of them, you can defy the natural order of things. (1 Corinthians 15:51-58) You have escaped the corruption that is in the world through lust. (James 1:13-15 / 1 Corinthians 10:13) You are partaking of the divine nature.

You Are (UR) -- profitable for ministry.

"The love of money is the root of all evil." (1 Timothy 6:10) There is no wiggle room here. Unfortunately, this Bible absolute is one that is not often talked about. But Paul the apostle reveals an equally telling truth in his requests before dying. Profitability is a powerful measure of all good.

Paul and John Mark had fallen out at Perga in Pamphylia. (Acts 13:13) Paul declared the basis of the dispute in Acts 15:36-38: It seems he thought it *"...not good to take him with them, who departed from them from Pamphylia, and went not with them to the work."* *"The work"* was all important to Paul, and evidently, John Mark, not unlike many before and after him, got distracted. Jesus is interested in the work, too. The master's anger in Matthew 25 (verses 24-30) was not at the wicked servant's balance sheet. It was at his confused slothfulness. And he called him "unprofitable."

Get it right now and never forget it. Men will endure, tolerate -- even forgive and elevate you as long as you make or save *(pronounced -- don't cost)* them money. But God and men will love and respect you as long as you demonstrate a clear understanding of and an unyielding commitment to *"the work."* Because both God and wise men know that focus, patience and persistence will soon cause your profiting to appear to all. (1 Timothy 4:15 / James 1:22-25 / 2 Timothy 4:1-5)

Paul called for John Mark at the end of his life. He must have gotten back on track. There is another truth here that bears noting. How you finish is critical. (Ezekial 33:1-16) John Mark finished well. And Paul characterized him as God sees you. You are profitable for ministry.

"Lose not courage, lose not faith, go forward."

Marcus Garvey

You Are (UR) --in for a taste treat.

NOVEMBER 5 *(PSALM 34:8)*

If you have yet to taste of the goodness of the Lord, don't wait another moment. He is good. Fleshly consumptions and indulgences can adversely affect the senses. What you believe filters what you hear, see, smell, feel and taste. Isaiah prophesied and Jesus identified that God would fatten hearts and make ears heavy and even shut the eyes of those who rebelled against him and chose the temporary comforts of earthly lusts over the eternal pleasures of His presence. (Isaiah 6:8-10 / Matthew 13:11-17)

How curious it is to be surrounded by good and not see it. (Jeremiah 17:5-9) To be overwhelmed with food and not taste or be filled with it. (2 Kings 7:1,2) To spend your life and get nothing of value in return. (Isaiah 55:1-3) You are in for a taste treat. O taste and see that the Lord is good!

You Are (UR) -- healed.

NOVEMBER 6 *(ISAIAH 53:3-5)*

(See also 1 Peter 2:24)
It's cooooold outside and a lot of folks are hacking, sniffling, and cough-ing. If you are one of them, remind the devil *(and all of his carefully named annoyances -- cold, cancer, etc...)* that Bible rules are like barber shop rules. *"First come - first served."*

Jesus understood it and applied it when the Pharisees challenged his au-thority. He said, *"Before Abraham was, I AM."* Now we can say it with the same authority. Before ????? was, I am -- Healed! Remember: bar-ber shop rules. *"You move -- you lose."*

You Are (UR) -- the sheep of His hand.

(PSALMS 95 & 23) NOVEMBER 7

You've read it and said it before -- perhaps as a Psalm of David. But David is dead and he watches among the great cloud of witnesses yearning for your manifestation as a son of God. (Hebrews 12:1,2 / Romans 8:19) **Say it out loud!**

The Lord is MY shepherd! I shall not want.
He makes me to lie down in green pastures.
He leads me beside the still waters. He restores my soul.
He leads me in the paths of righteousness for his name's sake.

Yea though I walk through the valley of the shadow of death
I will fear no evil: for thou art with me.
Thy rod and thy staff they comfort me.
Thou preparest a table before me in the presence of mine enemies.
Thou anointest mine head with oil. My cup runneth over.

Surely goodness and mercy shall follow me all the days of my life.
And I will dwell in the house of the Lord for ever.

You Are (UR) -- as a watered garden.

(JEREMIAH 31:10-12) NOVEMBER 8

It may seem odd to think of gardens as winter encroaches upon us, but in the realm of the Spirit, there is no better time. For it is God's great care for us that causes us to blossom in all seasons. Whether heat-withered drought or bitter cold, we can say like Paul, *"none of these things move me."* (Acts 20:22-35) Our source of nourishment, heat, refreshment and joy is not dependent upon nor subject to the forces that oppose us. We are not wild grasses or tumbleweeds, left to fend for ourselves. (Jeremiah 17:5-8) We are as a watered garden -- lovingly cared for by a watchful husbandman. (John 15:1-8)

You Are (UR) -- chosen.

NOVEMBER 9 *(JOHN 15:16)*

You got picked. You are on the team. (1 Peter 2:9) You get to go on the road trip. And believe it or not, you are in the big game. We need your contribution. We know you've got skills. But don't feel any pressure to perform, because we always win. (1 Cor. 15:57/2 Cor. 2:14)

Just rejoice that you got picked and your name is on the roster. (Luke 10:17-20) Folks are cheering for you. (Hebrews 12:1,2) And yes, you get a ring and a trophy when we win. (2 Timothy 4:6-8) WOW! HOORAY! YOU GO 'HEAD! Don't miss the bus.

You Are (UR) -- your ways.

NOVEMBER 10 *(HAGGAI 1:1-7)*

Perhaps you've said, or heard others say, *"I love her. I just don't like her ways."* This line of thinking is often associated with a *"no dealings"* social policy similar to the one between the Jews and the Samaritans. (John 4:9) We know we are called upon to love our neighbor as ourselves, but considering the behavior of some people, we may echo the rich young ruler in asking, *"Who is my neighbor?"*

After all, the scriptures do say, *"If it be possible, as much as lieth in you, live peaceably with all men."* (Romans 12:18) The questions become then: *"What is possible? And how much is really in us?"* And let us not forget that many of us judge others by their actions, while asking others to judge us by our intentions. So if, *"Even a child is known by his doings,"* as Solomon said, (Proverbs 20:11) then we have a dilemma. Because, like it or not, you are your ways.

You Are (UR) -- a fish out of water.

(EXODUS 2:9) NOVEMBER 11

Moses had no contemporaries. There were very few Israeli boys in his graduating class. At first glance, you may think it was because he was adopted by Pharoah's daughter and raised in Pharoah's palace. But think again. The deeper and ostensibly more compelling truth is that Pharoah had ordered all Hebrew males slaughtered at the time of Moses' birth. (Exodus 1:8-16) Like Jesus. (Matthew 2:1-17) Like so many among you and me. The deliverer had no playmates.

Had it not been for the grace, sovereignty, and mercy of God, coupled with the passion of the midwives and the defiance of his mother, Moses would have been just another casualty of war. But God is gracious. And the midwives were passionate. *(May these words add to the herarldry of their houses.)* Finally, Moses' mother was defiant, seeing that he was a *"goodly"* child, and she put him in the ark of bulrushes and deposited him in the Nile.

From day one, Moses was out of place. A, proverbial, fish out of water. Pharoah's daughter named him Moses because she *"drew him out of the water."* Consider the grace of God that moved her to ignore her father and pay the baby's own mother to nurse him. Consider the strange, strained relationship between Moses and Pharoah as the boy played with the prince of Egypt in the palace, daily defying the decree.

Moses' situation reminds me of Julius Caesar's comments to Antony concerning Cassius. *"Yond Cassius has a lean and hungry look. He thinks too much: such men are dangerous."*

It troubled Caesar that Cassius was a non-conformist. He didn't follow the crowd, as it were. And that made him a threat. It troubled Pharoah that there was such a crowd of Israelites in Egypt. The Jews have never been great assimilators and Moses was destined to be the least conforming ever. What an odd duck he must have been. Neither Egyptian nor Hebrew, Moses was a fish out of water, doomed *(or destined)* to be alone in a crowd.

You Are (UR) -- a fish out of water.

NOVEMBER 12 *(EXODUS 2:9)*

"Would that he (Cassius) were fatter!" Caesar said of Cassius. *"He reads much. He is a great observer, and he looks quite through the deeds of men. He loves no plays, as thou dost, Antony; he hears no music. Seldom he smiles, and smiles in such a sort as if he mocked himself and scorned his spirit that could be moved to smile at anything."* Then Caesar repeats my favorite line. *"Such men are dangerous."* Dangerous indeed.

Had Moses loved the dainties of Egypt more, he would have posed Pharoah no danger. But, alas, his allegiance was divided.

US Passports address the peculiar conflicts of *"Dual Nationals."* A person is considered a dual national when he owes allegiance to more than one country at the same time. Moses found himself greatly conflicted when he witnessed the cruel treatment that *"his brethren,"* the Hebrews, suffered at the hands of the Egyptians.

I can't believe that Moses had never witnessed such behavior before. It is easy, however, to believe that he had never actually *"seen"* their suffering. How many of us have had our eyes opened to the horrors the devil inflicts on *"our"* people, when we ourselves were enjoying his dainties, and spared the pain because of their patience, labor and prayers?

When Moses finally tried to *"do"* something, he was confronted with his identity crisis. Moses slew the Egyptian that he had witnessed smiting his Hebrew brother and hid his body. But the next day, when he attempted to break up a quarrel between two Israelis, they turned on him.

"Who made thee a prince and judge over us?
Intendest thou to kill me, as thou killedst the Egyptian?"

Moses was a man without a country, just as you and I are pilgrims and sojourners in this land. You are a fish out of water.

You Are (UR) -- a fish out of water.

(EXODUS 2:9) NOVEMBER 13

Consider the conflicted faith of our forefathers, those who sprang out of Abraham, Isaac, Jacob, and yes -- Moses.

"These all died in faith, not having received the promises, but having seen them afar off, and were persuaded of them, and embraced them, and confessed that they were strangers and pilgrims on the earth. For they that say such things declare plainly that they seek a country. And truly, if they had been mindful of that country from whence they came out, they might have had opportunity to have returned. But now they desire a better country, that is, an heavenly: wherefore God is not ashamed to be called their God: for he hath prepared for them a city."
Hebrews 11:13-16

For all its tensions, the story of Moses has a semi-happy ending. Moses delivered the children out of the hand of their oppressors. He led them through the wilderness and interceded for them, time and again, averting the wrath of God.

But at the end, no one attended Moses' funeral but God. And it is God, alone, who knows where to visit his grave. A fish out of water until the end, Moses had the same choice you and I have. He could befriend the world and become an unfruitful enemy of God. Or he could love God, embrace his calling and deliver his people.

"And have you not received faculties which will enable you to bear all that happens to you? Have you not received greatness of spirit? Have you not received courage? Have you not received endurance?"

Epictetus

You Are (UR) -- expected.

NOVEMBER 14 *(PROVERBS 18:16)*

We are in the thick of the *"holiday season"* and many of you will be traveling. Some will stay with relatives and friends, while others will enjoy the comforts of our nation's varied resorts, hotels, motels, B&B's and inns. Whatever your lodgings, if people know you're coming, you can be sure they are making room for you.

Should you neglect to call and cancel your arrangements, there will be consequences. You will have to face the ire of disappointed friends and family, or, with most major hoteliers, you will have to face the principal and interest of charged credit cards.

You are expected in the Spirit as well. Your gift(s) are making room for you. Just as surely as the great woman of 2 Kings 4 had her husband build a room for Elijah and compelled the prophet to come into her house at every opportunity, room is being made for you. Neglect not your gift(s). (1 Timothy 4:11-16) You are expected.

You Are (UR) -- a friend.

NOVEMBER 15 *(PROVERBS 27:5,6)*

I play golf. All too often, a problem occurs in my swing, and it can be extremely frustrating. The odd thing is, I usually can't figure out what's wrong on my own and I certainly can't figure it out on the golf course.

I have to go to the practice range and ask a teacher or a proficient friend what they see. It is their ability to see what's wrong, their willingness to say what's wrong and their eagerness to suggest ways to fix what's wrong that get me back to enjoying the game. Sometimes it hurts, but faithful are the wounds of a friend.

You Are (UR) -- a comforter.

(2 Cor. 1:1-5) NOVEMBER 16

The word comforter probably evokes one of two thoughts. The Holy Spirit is a comforter, helping our infirmities and making intercession for us with groanings that cannot be uttered. (John 14:15-17/Romans 8:28) And then there are those warm, fluffy, snuggly, bed covers that surround us on cold mornings. *(Bed, Bath & Beyond)* Neither one is bad, except for the fact that none of us can afford to stay in the bed all day. And that's where you come in.

Now people can experience the help and intercession of the Holy Spirit as well as the warm, fluffy, snuggly surroundings of an overstuffed covering while they make their way through a world that's getting colder by the minute. The natural comforter keeps them in the bed because it's filled with down. But God is at work in you and you are filled with up. (Philippians 2:12,13)

PS Solomon saw a world where the power was on the side of the oppressor and the oppressed had no comforter. There are people around you who see the same world, making the comfort you bring that much more -- comforting. (Ecclesiastes 4:1-3)

You Are (UR) -- older than Methuselah.

(Genesis 5:21-27) NOVEMBER 17

Say it with me. *"Old is good."* Hey! It beats the alternative. But I'm talking about an aging process that you may not have considered. Methuselah's daddy was Enoch. The scriptures say that he had this testimony, that he *"walked with God: and he was not; for God took him."* Now that's old. The man never died. You walk with God. He is coming to take you too. Jesus said it to Mary and Martha and he says it to you. You live and believe and you shall *"never see death."* (John 11:25,26)

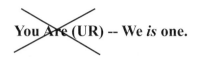

You Are (UR) -- We *is* one.

NOVEMBER 18 *(GENESIS 11:6)*

I know it's bad grammar. But it sure is good preaching.

From time to time, you will find words italicized in the King James Version of the Bible. This simple font change was the translators' admission that they were not altogether certain about their translation. Genesis 11:6 is especially interesting, in this regard, because it is easy to see the the the translators' struggle. Here you have a group of people that are on one accord. They had one language and one speech. They had one objective -- one goal. They intended to build a tower to God.

The force of their unity got God's attention. The scriptures say God *"came down to see...."* It was His response to their unity that stumped the translators. God said, *"Behold, the people is one."* The noun, "people," is plural, but the indefinite pronoun, "one," is singular. So what verb does a translator use?

They used the singular form of the living God's own name:
the verb "to be," often translated "I AM" or, in this case, "IS."

Truly the peoples' unity endued them with the power and presence of God. Jesus said, *"where two or three are gathered together in my name, there AM I in the midst of them."* (Matthew 18:19,20) That is why God ordered the relationship between man and wife so that the two would become one flesh. (Genesis 2:24) And he declared that the man who finds a wife has found a *"good thing,"* and that such men would obtain *"favor"* of the Lord. (Proverbs 18:22)

Well, we have been *"found"* by the bridegroom himself. We *is* walking in God's favor. We *is* part of the body of Christ. We *is* a member of the family of God. We *is* surrounded by a great cloud of witnesses. We *is* not ever alone.

I know it's bad grammar, but it is filled with power because it is filled with unity. We, my friends, *is* one.

You Are (UR) -- a slice of baloney.

(GALATIANS 3:28) NOVEMBER 19

Well, some may say that you are a slice of Ham or Shem or Japheth. Because somewhere, after Noah's drunken stupor at the landing of the ark, someone got the Darwinian notion that humanity evolved in separate strands from these three sons -- not just racially but hierarchically. And to that I say -- baloney!

Because of the curse of Canaan, (Genesis 9:20-24) these pseudo-separation scientologists would have us believe that brown-skinned people are sovereignly subservient to whoever donned their shores with Bibles and bullets first. And give or take a few marches and amendments, not much has changed since Noah -- at least not in America's churches.

The majority of Protestant churches in America are predominately, if not completely, segregated. It has been my experience, *(Quite extensive after publishing a book on the subject in 1991:* **One Nation Under Attack...*Understanding the creation of the nations)* that the ones that are not segregated, tend to model the nation in merely achieving desegregation, which is, all too often, naively mistaken for integration. And, in my humble opinion, even integration would not be enough.

What I would like to see, because I genuinely believe it is what the Lord would like to see, is a concept that can be described only by a word not yet in our lexicon.

Oneation: (See Ephesians 2:11-18)

> one•ate /'wƏn-at / *vb* ated; - ating *vt* **1:** to make one or unify <the body must be *oneated* ... that there be no schism or division, then no second line of defense will be needed. -- M. E. Evans > **2a:** to become one flesh < ≈ the man and his wife > **b:** to be: I AM < when *oneation* has occurred, "...the people *is* one" > to oneate -- derived from Jesus' command in Acts 1:8 and God's observation in Genesis 11:6

At the end of the day, Paul was right. There is neither Jew nor Greek. We are all one in Christ Jesus -- not just racially, but hierarchically, too. My pastor used to say, *"Life is like a sandwich. There will always be someone over you and there will always be someone under you. You, my friend, are just that slice of baloney in the middle."*

You Are (UR) -- moving.

NOVEMBER 20 *(GENESIS 12:1)*

If you're like me, you hate to move. Packing. Throwing things out. Ending relationships and establishing new ones. The truth is, we hate change, especially when the change involves the unknown.

Abram's whole life was upended by a single word from God.

> *"Get thee out of thy country, and from thy kindred, and from thy father's house, unto a land that I will shew thee."*

How strange that the God who changes not, brings about so much change into the lives of everyone He touches. But therein lies the key. We are moving toward Him -- the unmoveable, unshakeable foundation stone. Every change is an effort to be more like Him. And that removes one great unknown.

We may not know where we're going or how we'll get there, but we know that He will never leave us nor forsake us. John said, *"These things have I written unto you that believe on the name of the Son of God; that you may know that you have eternal life."* At least we know that wherever He's going is better than where we were going before we heard the word from Him. You've heard people say, *"God is moving."* If He's moving, we're moving.

You Are (UR) -- pregnant.

NOVEMBER 21 *(HEBREWS 11:11)*

It didn't just happen either. It required time, intimacy, strength and faith. *"Through faith...Sara herself received strength to conceive seed."* Sara also *"delivered"* a child. Will you trust God to bring forth that which is in you also?

You Are (UR) -- regaining a lot.

(GENESIS 14:12-16) NOVEMBER 22

Abram was missing a lot. His nephew, Lot, to be specific, along with Lot's family and all his possessions. Here's how Abram got it all back.

First, he made a decision. Indecision impedes action. It can even be evil and stop God's grace in our lives. (Matthew 6:22-24) *"For he that wavereth is like a wave of the sea driven with the wind and tossed. A double-minded man is unstable in all his ways."* (James 1:6,7)

Once his decision was made, Abram solicited the aid of loyal people-- people he had taken the time to foster relationships with. Each of these people had a servant's heart. They were well trained, totally trusted and fully equipped.

Finally, Abram did something that few men are able to do. He divided himself. He became Abram^{318} *(Abram to the 318th power.)*

A lot of what all of us are missing is due to the frailties and limitations of the flesh. Face it, we can't be in but one place at a time. Or can we? We can if we foster healthy relationships with people with hearts to serve. We can if we are willing to train them, equip them, and trust them. We can divide ourselves as Abram did and regain a lot.

You Are (UR) -- seen and heard of God.

(GEN. 16/21:9-21) NOVEMBER 23

Hagar was a victim of the doubts of others. Sarah chose Hagar, as a surro-gate, to conceive seed from Abraham. But when she did her duty she was despised and disowned. But God saw her wanderings and heard the voice of her child. And he promised to bless the seed. Some things in our lives are the seed of others' choices. But God sees us and hears our cry.

You Are (UR) -- getting fat.

NOVEMBER 24 *(PSALM 65:11)*

Wait! Before you panic and start reaffirming your resolution to shed the holiday pounds, consider the benefits. Think like a Christian. You are a citizen of heaven, not an American with a Victorian secret. Say it with me. *"Fat is good."* Fat is healthy. Fat is blessed. Fat is free from worry and anxiety sickness and disease. *(In the Spirit -- that is.)*

The diligent soul shall be made fat -- diligent and soul being the operative words. (Proverbs 13:4) Eli was heavy and could not control his appetites or his undisciplined sons of Belial. His eyesight grew dim and it was in his day that the Ark of God was taken from Israel. It seems that the fat of this world killed him. (1 Samuel 2:11-4:18 / Isaiah 6:9,10)

But you are not of this world. You are not a sluggard. Your heart is fixed and trusting in God. Your paths drop fatness and your *(spiritual)* heart is enlarged. (2 Corinthians 6:11) Happy holidays. You are getting fat.

You Are (UR) -- full.

NOVEMBER 25 *(EPHESIANS 3:14-21)*

It's the day after Thanksgiving and most people are stuffed. But you were full before you saw the turkey. Merciful. Graceful. Peaceful. Beautiful. Filled with the Spirit of the Most High God. Turkey and its triptopan will soon be gone. God and His goodness will always cause your cup to run over.

You Are (UR) -- working your buts off.

(HEBREWS 12:1,2) NOVEMBER 26

No, that's not some disgusting typo. I'm talking about those heavy, doubt-filled interjections that slow down God's plan for our lives. *"But I don't speak well."* Moses. *"But I'm just a child."* Jeremiah. *"But I'm old and my wife is barren."* Abraham. You get my drift.

We play a theatre game called, *"Yes and...."* The object is to agree with and encourage people. You lose if you stop the forward motion of the dialogue.

God says, *"I have made you the head and not the tail."* And a winner will say, *"Yes and I will give you all the glory by telling others."* God says; *"By my stripes you were healed."* And a winner will say, *"Yes and I shall live and not die and proclaim the works of the Lord."*

But, a loser might say, *"But what about this or what about that?"* And the conversation comes to a screeching halt. That's why we are working our 'buts' off.

You Are (UR) -- a child of promise.

(ROMANS 9:1-8) NOVEMBER 27

Isaac was a miracle long before he was born. It is difficult to imagine him being worried about anything. Even his father, Abraham, understood the magnitude of God's promise concerning this special son. (Hebrews 11:17) You, too, are a child of promise. God's promises can't come true if the difficulties overcome you. So face the difficulties in the comfort of the promise and walk in the faith of father Abraham. You are a child of promise.

You Are (UR) -- causing others to worship.

NOVEMBER 28 *(GENESIS 24:1-26)*

I hate shopping for other people. Even if you think you know them well, there is simply no accounting for taste. So imagine the pressure Abraham's servant felt when he was charged to find a wife for Isaac, his master's son.

That senior steward had learned some valuable lessons from his master, Abraham, and the first thing he did was pray. It is amazing to eavesdrop as he sets the criteria for his choice.

> *"O Lord God of my master Abraham, I pray thee, send me good speed this day, and shew kindness unto my master Abraham. Behold, I stand here by the well of water; and the daughters of the men of the city come out to draw water: And let it come to pass, that the damsel to whom I shall say, Let down thy pitcher, I pray thee, that I may drink; and she shall say, Drink, and I will give thy camels drink also: let the same be she that thou hast appointed for thy servant Isaac, and thereby shall I know that thou hast shewed kindness unto my master."*

Father Abraham was looking for a servant who would go beyond that which was requested. Aren't we all? Make no mistake, Rebecca was beautiful. So beautiful, in fact, that Isaac lived to face the same fears that his father had concerning Sarah. (See Genesis 12:10-20 & 26:6,7) But it was Rebecca heart (the heart of a true servant) that made the difference.

Rebecca was the answer to his prayer in grand fashion, providing water for him and his camels and then offering lodging, straw and provender in her father's house. Her generosity moved the servant to bow down and worship the Lord.

Each time you turn the other cheek, go the second mile and in true Macedonian fashion, "willing of yourselves," go "beyond your power," you cause others to worship. (1 Corinthians 8:1-5)

You Are (UR) -- choosing your children.

(DEUT. 30:15-20) NOVEMBER 29

People pit the *"right to choose"* against the *"right to life"* as though they were, somehow, mutually exclusive. The truth is, every choice we make impacts our lives. And every choice we make impacts the lives of our children.

Now you may say, *"I don't have any children."* I would retort, perhaps slightly unfairly, *"case in point."* And to the advocate of abortion who might say, *"A woman should have the right to choose."* I say boldly, without hesitation, *"if only your mother had."* But I digress.

You see, somewhere, in my fuzzy past, I remember a philosophy that was characterized by the mantra *"Do it for the children."* It was a philosophy of self-sacrifice. It was a philosophy of forward thinking. It was a philosophy of hope.

It was why my mother and father stayed together through things my sister and I have yet to develop the willingness, ability, or perhaps, sadly, the character to tolerate in our marriages. It is why, at 98 years of age, my wife's grandmother, Sadie Utley, gets up everyday before sunrise and cooks homemade biscuits, and is a little bit peeved if you don't get up to eat them. It was why my Aunt Clara didn't spend all the money she made on herself, but gave me, her church, and a few other chosen individuals, two or three years of her income *(each)* throughout her life and then left me at least one year's salary when she died.

In this age of indignant individualism, we seem to be willingly ignorant of the concept of cause and effect. We throw around misnomers like *"victimless crime,"* *"self-made man,"* and *"innocent victims."*

Balderdash!

We are all creatures of choice. We are where we are, we have what we have, and we have become what we have become, because of our choices. We have chosen (Joshua 24:15) and we have been chosen. (John 15:16) And now we are challenged to choose -- our children.

You Are (UR) -- changing your children.

NOVEMBER 30 *(1 Kings 3:16-28)*

The wisdom of Solomon is legendary, and it was presented to the world for the first time in a choice concerning a child. Two harlots had babies, three days apart. They were roommates and one rolled over on her sleeping child and the baby died. When she awakened to the horror in the middle of the night, she switched the babies and hoped against hope that her roommate wouldn't notice. But mothers know and they went to the king to settle their dispute.

"Divide the living child in two, and give half to the one , and half to the other," was the king's decree. Any mother knows, that the living child's mother would rather give her son to a liar than have him slain, which is what she begged the king to do. In so doing, she revealed the truth to Solomon.

Change. Her roommate changed the children. The living child's mother offered to exchange her custodial rights for the life of her son. Everyone involved was changed forever. You are changing your children.

You Are (UR) -- charging your children.

DECEMBER 1 *(2 Timothy 4:1-5)*

"Charge" is one of those peculiar words that can be applied in a variety of ways and has shifted in usage over time. The essence of its meaning, however, remains consistent. **Charge:** *a material weight or load of obligation or responsibility.* We are charging our children with a standard of honor to maintain or a debt of honor to regain.

You Are (UR) -- chauffeuring your children.

(1 Corinthians 7:14) DECEMBER 2

My daughter was two years old the first time she flew on an airplane. We were waiting at the terminal as the crew prepared for departure, and all was well until we started to taxi. We didn't know how Gabrielle would react, but this is what she said.

"Airplane's moving." "Yeah sweetie," I said, *"it's taking us to see Mickey Mouse."* We were going to San Diego on business and then to Disneyland. I hoped the reminder would assuage her fear. Gabrielle looked around calmly at me, her mother, and my secretary *(the three people who had been chauffeuring her everywhere, all of her short life)* and she asked one profound question. *"Who's driving?"*

Your children are riding with you. You are driving them everywhere they will go. Not just to soccer practice and dance recitals, but to or away from God. They are riding, literally, on the coattails of your righteousness. *"Who's driving?"* You're driving. You are chauffeuring your children.

You Are (UR) -- cheering your children.

(2 Timothy 1:1-7) DECEMBER 3

Everybody needs a good pep rally from time to time, especially when they're on a losing streak. And we all experience losing streaks. If you have children, you are the default head cheerleader. So embrace it.

I once heard a famous but seemingly troubled comedian say, *"My dad was an accountant. If he had hugged me just once, I would probably be an accountant today."* Wealth and fame have their place I suppose, but true success is measured in relationships. So get your megaphone and your pom poms and turn a few back flips. Rah, Rah, Sis-Boom-Bah. Whether you're ma or whether you're pa. You are cheering your children.

You Are (UR) -- cheating your children.

DECEMBER 4 *(JUDGES 11)*

"Jephtha vowed a vow unto the Lord, and said, If thou shalt without fail deliver the children of Ammon into mine hands, then it shall be, that whatsoever cometh forth of the doors of my house to meet me, when I return in peace from the children of Ammon, shall surely be the Lord's, and I will offer it up for a burnt offering." (vss 30,31)

Sounds great, until you consider that Jephtha is offering to pay for something that God has already promised. And he's bargaining with a life that is not his own. Too often the sacrifices we make "for" our children, are really made "with" our children, when a little confidence is all that is needed.

You Are (UR) -- a chosen child.

DECEMBER 5 *(ROMANS 8:14,15)*

I wrote about adoption on August 26 but shortly thereafter, I was reminded of something wonderful. A couple in our church called to say that they wouldn't be at service Sunday morning. They had been preparing, for months, to adopt a baby. When one agency took too long, they went to a second agency and both agencies called with babies on the same day. One, a toddler, was described as a *"jolly little fellow who had never met his mother."* The other had just been born when they called and they were going to pick him up.

The wonder of the Spirit of Adoption came alive for me again. *(We adopted our daughter when she was seven months old.)* When I held this chosen child and beheld his chosen parents, I could only marvel at the grace of God. *"Before I formed thee in the belly I knew thee; and before thou camest forth out of the womb I sanctified thee,"* he told Jeremiah. He says the very same thing to us. You are a chosen child. (John 15:16)

You Are (UR) -- challenging your children.

(JEREMIAH 1:1-10) DECEMBER 6

It is said that rivers are crooked because they avoid trouble. Especially in early tributary stages *(childhood)*, glistening streams and babbling brooks trickle around rocks and trees. As they grow older, however, they strengthen and straighten. Young men, on the other hand, tend to avoid trouble and grow crooked unless they are challenged to face their fears by those they love, trust, and respect.

Jeremiah, for example, tried to use his youth as an excuse. Dodging the challenges of the responsibility that God called him to, he said, *"I cannot speak: for I am a child."* He could not have known, however, that his very choice of words heralded the presence of God. *"I AM a child."*

God ignored Jeremiah's excuses and challenged him not to despise his youth. (1 Timothy 4:12) And He challenged him with the foreordinance of his future. *"Before I formed thee in the belly I knew thee; and before thou camest forth out of the womb I sanctified thee, and I ordained thee a prophet unto the nations."* You are challenging your children.

You Are (UR) -- trees of righteousness.

(ISAIAH 61:1-3) DECEMBER 7

Christmas is getting closer. It's time to decorate the tree. I'm not talking about that fir or cedar in your living room. I'm talking about the you God has called you to be.

It's time to deck your halls with beauty. It's time to don the garment of praise. It's time to sing the Yuletide carrol that Jesus is crucified, buried, and raised.

You Are (UR) -- renovating.

DECEMBER 8 *(3 John 2)*

All renovations begin with an idea -- a mental picture of what should or could be. Whether it is a restoration to original splendor or the revelation of some new thing, everything begins with a dream.

So goes the renovation of your life. You have to see it inside before you can be it outside. And there is a direct corollary from your soul's condition to your goal's position.

David expressed this marvelously when he said, *"I will praise thee; for I am fearfully and wonderfully made: and that my soul knoweth right well."* (Psalm 139:14) You are renovating, and the blueprints are in your soul.

You Are (UR) -- at liberty to flee.

DECEMBER 9 *(Daniel 3)*

King Nebuchadnezzar was so angry at the rebellion of Shadrach, Meshach, and Abednego, that he overheated his furnace just to kill them. It was so hot, in fact, that the men who were order to put them into the furnace, died the moment the door was opened. And the three Hebrew boys were free. They were at liberty to flee. But they didn't. They went on in.

The king was astonished to see a *"fourth"* man in the furnace with them as they walked about suffering no harm. And then, irony of ironies, the king had to ask them to come out of the death chamber he had sentenced them to.

You too are free. You are at liberty to flee. You can leave at any time. But the glory is far greater when your deliverance arrives, if you are found faithful, waiting for the Father, with the Son.

You Are (UR) -- stretching the truth.

(MATT. 14:13-21) DECEMBER 10

What you have is good. But it is not enough. What you know is true. But it has yet to travel from the "good book" to your checkbook, pocketbook, datebook -- or any other book that chronicles your life. You have the 'problem' of Jabez. You need to be blessed indeed. You need your coast enlarged. You need to stretch the truth.

God is a master at stretching that which is not enough. He takes a word of truth and makes it cover a world of need. Of Moses he asked, *"What is that in thine hand?"* Of the Shunamite widow he asked, *"What hast thou in the house?"* When asked for a morsel of bread by the prophet, the widow of Zarephath declared that she had only "an handful of meal in a barrel, and a little oil in a cruse." She planned to share this last meal with her son and die. But God stretches the truth.

Jesus took five loaves and two fish and stretched a meal for two into a feast for thousands -- with leftovers! He declared that *"greater works than these"* shall we do. The truth is:

The truth is; what you have is good. But it is not enough. What you know is true. But it has yet to travel from the "good book" to your checkbook, pocketbook, datebook -- or any other book that chronicles your life. You have the 'problem' of Jabez. You need to be blessed indeed. You need your coast enlarged. You need to stretch the truth.

You Are (UR) -- working.

(PROVERBS 14:23) DECEMBER 11

Doesn't matter what you're doing. (Provided it's not unrighteous.) In all labor there is profit. Don't bemoan the profile. Don't curse the routine. Thank God that you're working and expect a profit soon.

You Are (UR) -- death defiant.

DECEMBER 12 *(ROMANS 8:1,2)*

Say it out loud!

I am not afraid of dying. Death has no power over me.
The law of life in Christ Jesus -- indeed has set me free.
Free from the law of sin and death. I walk not after the flesh.
I follow after the Spirit. I'm saved. I'm healed. I'm blessed.

I overcome the devil -- by my testimony and Christ's blood.
The Spirit shall lift up a standard against the enemy
when he comes in like a flood.
Flee you demons and devils. I am submitted to the Lord most high.
To live is Christ. He has hid my life. And I gain even if I die.

But I shall not die. I shall not die -- but live and His works declare.
I am death defiant. For nothing shall I care.
I shall not die. I shall not die. With long life I'll be satisfied.
I am death defiant. For I serve the one who died.

(2 Timothy 1:7 / Romans 10:13 / 2 Peter 2:24 / Galatians 3:13,14 / Revelation 12:7-11 / Isaiah 59:19 / James 4:7 / Philippians 1:21 / Colossians 3:1-4 / Psalm 118:17 / Philippians 4:6-8 / Psalm 91:16 / Romans 7:24,25)

You Are (UR) -- God's delight.

DECEMBER 13 *(PROVERBS 11:20)*

There is nothing as fulfilling as a father's smile. Imagine what Jesus must have felt when God said, *"This is my beloved son in whom I am well pleased."* Men and women all over the world have amassed fortunes, acquired treasures, accepted accolades and achieved what seemed impossible yet remain unfulfilled because dad does not or cannot approve. But our heavenly Father approves. Not only does God delight in our uprightness, but He delights in the mercy that is required to keep us that way. (Micah 7:18,19) You are God's delight.

You Are (UR) -- called to lend.

(DEUTERONOMY 28) DECEMBER 14

America is trillions of dollars in debt. Families average tens of thousands of dollars in credit card bills that will undoubtedly increase as we approach the Christmas holiday. So it may be difficult to imagine yourself lending to many nations. But imagining is where it begins.

You were created in God's image. He imagined you lending to many nations and borrowing from none. You are Abraham's seed and an heir according to the blessing. You are called to lend.

You Are (UR) -- not a thief.

(PROVERBS 30:7-9) DECEMBER 15

Tempted to steal? I'm not talking about armed robbery or car jacking. That would be far too dramatic and the consequences too immediate. No, I'm talking about the common, everyday, widely accepted, practice of not paying your tithes.

Your pastor doesn't preach it? The money is still the Lord's and He was not unclear about where He wanted it taken. *"Bring ye all the tithes into the storehouse,"* is what He said. (Malachi 3:8-10) *"Old Testament,"* you say? *"Under the law,"* you say? **Remember:** Levi, who received tithes, payed tithes in Abraham to Mechisedek before there was a law. (Hebrews 7:1-10)

The bottom line is, you are not a thief. *"Thou shalt not steal,"* was a prophetic commandment concerning those who would one day have the law written in their hearts and in their minds. (Hebrews 10:16,17) It was a prophetic commandment concerning you. And you are not a thief.

You Are (UR) -- making a living.

DECEMBER 16 *(LUKE 15:11,12)*

More than money. More than things. You are making a living. You are establishing the principals and concepts that will provide for your family and contribute to your world for generations to come. Every gift you develop. Every talent you perfect. Every lesson you convey. Every standard you impart. You are making a mark that cannot be erased. You are making a living.

You Are (UR) -- a success.

DECEMBER 17 *(JOHN 14:12)*

So who is your successor? When Jesus declared *"It is finished,"* (John 19:30) He was referring to His payment of our debt of sin. But you will notice that the Lord of glory stuck around a while after that. Because although *"it"* was finished, He wasn't yet finished. Jesus knew what all great leaders know. No one is a success without a successor.

After His resurrection, Jesus asked for His disciples and Peter, in particular. He comissioned them to preach the gospel and gave them the power to remit or retain sins. (John 20:19-23)

They were charged to cast out devils, lay hands on the sick, and speak with new tongues, under the leading and power of the Holy Spirit. (Mark 16:15-20) They were equipped to do the works that Jesus did and even *"greater works."*

Now Jesus was finished. Now He could depart. He counted His mission a success because He had not one, but one hundred and twenty successors. (Acts 1 / Acts 2)

You Are (UR) -- out of luck.

(PROVERBS 16:33) DECEMBER 18

Luck. I have often heard it called *"blessings from Lucifer."* Thank God, we are out of luck. Good, bad, Irish, or dumb, our blessings come from God. Break a mirror, while walking under a ladder, carrying a thirteen month old baby's black cat, stepping on cracks, all the way to a St. Patrick's day celebration, on Friday the thirteenth, and God will still know the number of the very hairs on your head. If you fall, He will raise you up. And when you get up, thank the God who saved you that you are out of luck.

You Are (UR) -- a wise fool.

(1 JOHN 2:12-14) DECEMBER 19

The proper word is sophomore. It's the second year. It's our adolescence. It's knowing just enough to think you know enough. It's a very dangerous place to be and the only way out is to *"overcome the wicked one."*

You don't wish it on anyone, but there are seasons in some of our lives when we must needs go through something. (1 Peter 1:6) David had his Goliath. Samson had his Delilah. There was a lion's den for Daniel, and a fiery furnace for Shadrach, Meshach, and Abednego.

Esther met Haman. The church met Paul. Nehemiah wouldn't come down off the wall. Jonah was swallowed. Paul was caught up. Peter was imprisoned. Even Jesus was *"in all points tempted like as we are, yet without sin."* (Hebrews 4:14,15)

One thing is certain, when your test comes, God will be expecting you to prevail with flying colors. He was rooting for Job. And the great cloud of witnesses is rooting for you. You may be a sophomore now, but graduation grows closer, day by day.

You Are (UR) -- flying solo.

DECEMBER 20 *(DANIEL 6:1-24)*

Daniel went into the lions' den alone -- or so it appeared. But a solo flight does not go unsupported. The angels of the Lord shut the lions' mouths. And much like the fourth man (the Son of God) was in the fiery furnace with Shadrach, Meshach, and Abednego, the presence of the angels caused Daniel to suffer no hurt. But someone else was attendant to Daniel's plight.

It seems that king Darius, the very man who made the decree that sentenced Daniel to the lion's den, was a less than willing participant in the affair. When he found he could not legally deliver Daniel from the den, the king assured Daniel that God -- the God of Daniel -- would deliver Daniel, and then the king spent the entire night in prayer and fasting. He was the first man on the scene to inquire about Daniel's condition. And he was delighted to see that Daniel slept well. Daniel was flying solo, but he was not alone.

You Are (UR) -- a guiding light.

DECEMBER 21 *(MATTHEW 2:1,2)*

"Now when Jesus was born in Bethlehem of Judaea in the days of Herod the king, behold, there came wise men from the east to Jerusalem, saying, 'Where is he that is born King of the Jews? for we have seen his star in the east, and are come to worship him.'"

Wise men still seek the King of kings. The only difference is, the light is no longer in the sky like some astrological sentinel. You are the light. The words that you speak and the works that you do are leading men to Jesus.

As you serve God and man, men come to worship Jesus. That is the true measure of your "Christmas Spirit," that all who come in your presence are moved to worship Him.

You Are (UR) -- God's gift.

(EPHESIANS 4:7-16) DECEMBER 22

If you are called to five-fold, full-time ministry, make these words your own. If you are not, let these words be a blessing to the shepherd God has placed in your life. Gifts should be treasured, not just for their inherent value, but for the value of the relationship that inspired them. God so loved the world, that He gave His only begotten son. God so loved the church, that He gave apostles, prophets, evangelists, pastors, and peachers. *"Thanks be to God for His unspeakable gift."* (2 Corinthians 9:15)

You Are (UR) -- invited to dinner.

(REVELATION 19:9,10) DECEMBER 23

Holidays are filled with food. That has always been one of my favorite parts. But parties can be social separators and half the battle is getting invited. So many people spend the holiday season depressed that they are not counted among the "beautiful people." Like Cinderella, they watch the wicked stepsisters prepare, because the prince is having a ball.

But there is one celebration that neither money, class, pedigree, nor station can avail you to. You are called to the marriage supper of the Lamb. There will be a great multitude of people there which no man can number, of all nations, and kindreds, and people, and tongues. The dress code is simple and standard: white robes with palms in your hand.

Everyone will follow the same protocol. Learn the salutation now. *"Amen: Blessing, and glory, and wisdom, and thanksgiving, and honour, and power, and might, be unto our God for ever and ever. Amen."* (Revelation 7:9-12)

Don't be depressed. Get dressed. You are called to the marriage supper of the Lamb.

You Are (UR) -- the reason for the season.

DECEMBER 24 (JOHN 18:37)

"Jesus is the reason for the season."

You will probably see and hear this popular jingle a lot during the Christmas holidays. And from one perspective it is true. But the reason Jesus came was *"to seek and to save that which was lost."* (Luke 19:10) The reason Jesus came -- was you.

You Are (UR) -- the Christ, the son of the living God.

DECEMBER 25 (MATTHEW 16:13-19)

When Simon Barjona declared this answer to Jesus' question concerning who He was, he had no way of knowing how that declaration would change his life. It was a revelation. The spirit of the living God had revealed the Messiah to a man.

It was on that day, with that revelation, that Jesus changed Simon's name. It was on that day, with that revelation, that Jesus changed Simon. *"Thou art Peter,"* Jesus said to this enlightened man. *"And upon this rock,"* (Jesus was not referring to Peter, whose new name is taken from the Greek root **petros** meaning detached pebble, easily thrown or moved - No! - Jesus was referring to the revelation that He is the Christ, from the Greek root **petra** meaning unshakeable, unmoveable, mass of foundation stone.)

"And upon this rock," He said, *"I will build my church; and the gates of hell shall not prevail against it. And I will give unto thee the keys of the kingdom of heaven: and whatsoever thou shalt bind on earth shall be bound in heaven: and whatsoever thou shalt loose on earth shall be loosed in heaven."*

That is Jesus' gift to you. He has made you part of that great revelation. He is the head and you are His body. He has given you the keys to the kingdom.

You Are (UR) -- in the beginning.

The beginning is not a point on a linear lifeline. The beginning is not a blip on a digital clock. The beginning is a living, breathing person who transcends time, and his name is Jesus.

> *"I am Alpha and Omega, the beginning and the ending,"* saith the Lord, *"which is, and which was, and which is to come, the Almighty."*

Once we understand that and believe that we are, in fact, "in him," (Acts 17:28) everything changes. *"In the beginning, God created."* There is creative power in Jesus. There is resurrection, healing, delivering, re-deeming power -- in Jesus. Whatever is missing, lacking, broken, ailing, dying, or even dead in you can be re-created -- in Jesus. You are in the beginning.

You Are (UR) -- in the beginning.

In the beginning was the Word. We are not talking about inanimate frag-ments of speech here. Just as "the beginning" is a person, "the Word" is that very same person. Spoken. Written. Living. Heard. Jesus is "the Word...made flesh." He dwelt among us and now we live in him.

The Word is the tool that God used to create the worlds. (Hebrews 11:3) "Without him (the Word) was not anything made that was made." That creative force fills us, surrounds us, infuses us. We are in him and he in us, and just as he and his Father are one, we are one in him. This three-fold cord is not easily broken. (Ecclesiastes 4:9-12) We are in the begin-ning.

You Are (UR) -- in the beginning.

DECEMBER 28 *(GENESIS 1)*

You are living in the realm -- yea, in the very person -- of God's declarations. *"In the beginning...God said."* Those declarations are *"sent"* (Romans 10:14-17) to establish authorized truth. They determine what IS. Regardless of what has become. What God says -- IS.

When God beheld the discombobulation of his creation, he declared the opposite of what he s-a-w. He declared what w-a-s. *"And God said, Let there be...."* Light. Life. Trees. Beasts. Fishes. Fowl. Man. God calls those things which be not, as though they were. He calls them so, because from where God sits -- they are.

Never forget: "God is not a man, that he should lie." (Numbers 23:19) He cannot lie, because once he says a thing, it becomes true. He is the truth. (John 14:6) So, "let God be true, but every man a liar." Every man who disagrees with God, that is. And that includes you. You are living in the realm of God's declarations. You are in the beginning.

You Are (UR) -- in the beginning.

DECEMBER 29 *(GENESIS 1:26-28)*

You are at the idea's source. You are in that perfect time and place called imagination, when, or where, God declared, *"Let us make man in our own image...."* God the Father, God the Son, and God the Holy Spirit, convened a holy triumvirate and imagined you. And Jesus is the express image of God's person, (Hebrews 1:1-4) the archetype, if you will.

In a world where things are but imperfect imitations of ideas, you abide in Jesus. You dwell in perfection. You live in that which God imagined. At a time when things seem "upside down" (Acts 17:6) and altogether backwards, you are in the beginning.

You Are (UR) -- breathing.

(PSALM 150) DECEMBER 30

Praise Him! It's a no brainer. Breathing. Praising. Thomas Cahill in his fascinating book *The Gifts of the Jews* *(not for the fainthearted)* makes a powerful case concerning the name of God. - YHWH - *"But for me,"* he says, *"when I attempt to say the consonants without resort to vowels, I find myself just breathing in, then out, with emphasis, in which case God becomes the breath of life."* Breathing. Praising. You are breathing.

You Are (UR) -- called to repentance.

(ACTS 2:37,38) DECEMBER 31

We have reached the end of another year and people are preparing to begin anew. On the morrow, resolutions will be made -- bold declarations of that which we intend to change. But in the words of Whitney Young, legendary civil rights leader and former Executive Director of the National Urban League: *"The danger is that people may mistake what is basically a change of vocabulary for a change in behavior, practices, and attitudes."*

Repentance, then, is first acknowledging that you are a sinner. We have not just done something wrong, but there are things about us that are wrong which cause us to do such things. Once that acknowledgement is made, we must ask God to forgive us. Only God can forgive us, and He expressed His willingness to forgive, when He gave His son, Jesus, for us. (John 3:16 / 1 John 3:16) Finally, we must be willing to change.

continued...

You Are (UR) -- called to repentance.

DECEMBER 31 *(CONTINUED)*

The changes that we make are not for the pleasure or approval of men. Though men may be pleased, we are driven by Godly sorrow. The sorrow that we have become something other than God intended. (2 Corinthians 7:8-10) We cry, as David did:

"Against thee, thee only, have I sinned, and done this evil in thy sight: that thou mightest be justified when thou speakest, and be clear when thou judgest. Behold, thou desirest truth in the inward parts: and in the hidden part thou shalt make me to know wisdom." (Psalm 51)

David dwelled in the secret place of the most high. David abode in the shadow of the Almighty. David said of the Lord, *"He is my refuge and my fortress: my God; in him will I trust."* (Psalm 91) David was a man after God's own heart. David mastered what we must resolve. We are called to repentance.

"Be strong and of a good courage: for unto this people shalt thou divide for an inheritance the land, which I sware unto their fathers to give them.

Only be thou strong and very courageous, that thou mayest observe to do according to all the law, which Moses my servant commanded thee: turn not from it to the right hand or to the left, that thou mayest prosper whithersoever thou goest."

Joshua 1:6,7

PRAISE FOR THE ENCOURAGEMINT

Every morning when I open my e-mail, there is an anointed delight waiting for me. It's The EncourgeMINT. Thoughtful and succinct, The EncourgeMINT is a daily meditation that helps keep me focused on and receptive to God's ordering of my footsteps. I keep my daily EncourgeMINTs in a file so I can revisit them when I want them (or need them & sometimes there's a difference) for myself, or to help with my witnessing to others.

When my feet get snagged among the briars of obstruction in my daily journey, and I'm distracted by the annoyances of the accuser from God's proof and purpose in my life, The EncourgeMINT helps me beat back the thorns and brambles. I hear God speak to me through The EncourgeMINT. It is too timely, too cogent, too right, too often to be anything other than an electronic whisper (or sometimes a cattle prod) to urge me on to do the things He would have me do as He continues to perfect His Word and will in my life. Michael, **You Are (UR)** *both blessed and a blessing.*

Roland Staton -- Durham, NC
Program Director -- GOTTA SAVE PROJECT, Inc.
A Community Development Corporation

The EncourageMINT will inspire all that read these wonderful words of wisdom. This is truly a work for all generations, especially for those who seek Him -- Jesus.

Donald Q. Fozard, Sr. -- Durham, NC
Pastor -- Mount Zion Christian Church

The EncourageMINT is a pleasant awakening every morning. Mr. Michael E. Evans has been an inspiration to us all in the words of Christ our savior.

Calvin B. Reed -- Charleston, SC
President -- AAA Financial Services

This book is the essence of the teaching style of my pastor, Michael E. Evans -- profound, honest, thought provoking, funny, engaging, motivating, convicting, yet encouraging. The EncourageMINT provides many "lightbulb moments."

Pastor Mike's teaching has blessed me immensely and it has touched every area of my life. I am so blessed as a result of the seed of the word sown. I am encouraged to keep growing in the Word of God. I hope you experience the same.

Carol S. Etheridge -- Charleston, SC
Director of Human Resources -- Orient Express Hotels, North America

PRAISE FOR THE ENCOURAGEMINT

Your daily inspirational messages keep me going. May God continue to bless you and your family.

Clay N. Middleton -- Camp Cooke / Al Taji, Iraq
2nd Lieutenant in charge of the Direct Signal Support Team (DSST)

I enjoy reading your daily EncourageMint e-mails. It's a great start to my day and on occasion I will forward a copy to others. It appears that your ministry has taken on a whole new direction and you are fulfilling God's purpose for your life. I commend you on your efforts. I pray for the success of your ministry and that God will continue to use you as an instrument to spread the Gospel of our Lord and Savior, Jesus Christ.

Herb Courtney -- Ambler, PA
M and T Bank

You better believe we want a book and an autographed one at that! (smile) We have been soooo encouraged with your e-mail over the years. Just to start our computer up each morning knowing that there was an encouraging word just for us has been a blessing. Theresa always said that this should have been put in book form so that we can reference back and now you have done just that. Bless you. We will (as always) continue to pass your information on.

Barry & Theresa Ross -- Conway, SC

It is my pleasure to recommend Mike Evans to you for a daily dose of mind massage. Mike brings years of reading, writing, thinking and living to this project. I have had the pleasure of watching Mike and Gloria work their way back toward all that God has for them. They truly have something of value to share with you through "The EncourageMINT!"

Chip Judd -- Georgetown, SC
Pastor -- Victory Christian Fellowship

Thanks so much for making me aware of your efforts in regard to this publication. I have enjoyed the few moments I have spent with it and appreciate its artful yet "to the point" approach. You are an encouragement and a blessing. Thanks brother.

Curtis E. Bostic -- Charleston, SC
Bostic Law Firm, PA

My God Pastor E. That (7/19) was just for me. An on time Word to keep me encouraged and focused. I trust that all is well with you and your bride and your little princess. I thank God often for you and pray that you will receive a full harvest for all the seeds that you sow into our lives. In Jesus Name, Amen.

Your brother in Christ,
Wallace Hunter -- Charleston, SC

PRAISE FOR THE ENCOURAGEMINT

The weekday nuggets from The EncourageMINT serve as inspiration and "spiritual food for thought". There is always something I can relate to, which causes me to examine my thoughts or situations through a different lens--It's a daily reminder to focus on God's way, God's truth and God's promises.

Stephanie M. Walker -- Greensboro, NC
Walker & Associates Consulting Inc.

Praise God and Hallelujah! All I can say is that I thank God for all of the words of wisdom He transfers through you as His instrument. I am still in the infant stages of the cyber-age, but I really do enjoy The EncourageMINT daily. God's blessings in all that you do, and a special blessing on your family and your congregation.

Linda Dingle Gadson -- Johns Island, SC
Executive Director -- Rural Missions, Inc.

The EncourageMINT always seems to speak to me when everything is going in the opposite direction. Early in the morning, it really encourages me.

Wilfred Fields -- Mount Pleasant, SC
Electrical Supervisor -- College of Charleston

Hey Michael:
I'm just taking the time to say "thank you" for your EncourageMINT(s). This one (5/29) really hit the mark. I appreciate what you are doing to build up Christ's Body. **You (UR) Are** *-- a true "bodybuilder."*

Blessings and Love,
JoAnn Parrott -- Charleston, SC

These messages have meant so much to me. Some days they are saying exactly what I need to hear at exactly the moment I need to hear it. Other days, they are saying exactly what I need to hear, but don't want to. (smile) Mostly, they have kept me in remembrance of a man who has been called, appointed, and anointed. One who has spoken into my life for several years now, and while you aren't my local pastor anymore, it is refreshing to see that you're allowing God to still use you to minister to His flock and more specifically to me.

Lydia Brooks -- Raleigh, NC

Thank you for these nuggets of Y-O-Uranium. I met you when you spoke at Highland church in NYC and am very glad to be on your mailing list.

Harold D! -- Jamaica Queens, NY

MAKING A MINT

The US Mint was established in April of 1792. Its primary mission is to produce an adequate volume of circulating coinage for the nation to conduct its trade and commerce. There are four such facilities in the country now:

The Philadelphia Mint, *Pennsylvania*: The engraving of U.S. coins and medals; production of medal and coin dies; production of coins of all denominations for general circulation; production of regular uncirculated coin sets; production of commemorative coins authorized by Congress; production of medals; the conducting of public tours and maintenance of the facility's sales center.

The Denver Mint, *Colorado*: Production of coins of all denominations for general circulation; production of coin dies; production of regular uncirculated coin sets; production of commemorative coins authorized by Congress; the conducting of public tours and maintenance of the facility's sales center; storage of gold and silver bullion.

The San Francisco Mint, *California*: Production of regular proof coin sets in clad and silver; production of selected commemorative coins authorized by Congress.

The West Point Mint, *New York*: Production of all uncirculated and proof one-ounce silver bullion coins, all sizes of the uncirculated and proof American Eagle gold bullion and platinum bullion coins; production of all silver, gold, platinum, and bi-metallic commemorative coins authorized by Congress; storage of silver, gold, and platinum bullion.

On January 1 of 2003 a new mint was established:

The EncourageMINT, *South Carolina*: Production of words, fitly spoken, for the body of Christ to conduct its trade and commerce. Our efforts are authorized by God. In Him we trust. Faith, courage, and confidence are the coin of the realm. (Hebrews 11:1-6 / 1 Samuel 30:1-6 / 1 John 3:19-22)

You Are (UR) -- greatly appreciated.

(Philippians 4:10-19) THANKS

This is a curious vocation that we have -- preaching the gospel. Helping people to Find, Follow, and Finish their courses in life is, indeed, a high and holy calling. Whether in business or ministry, however, it is often undervalued. **Remember:** *"Advice unsolicited is usually unheeded."* So when people get it -- it is greatly appreciated. And as Paul told the Philippians, you get it. *(My paraphrase.)*

Coming to church and paying your tithes and offerings. (Hebrews 10:16-25 / Malachi 3:6-8) Invitations to preach at other churches. (Acts 16:9,10) Calls to speak at business retreats and conferences. (1 Corinthians 9:1-11) Opportunities to train your groups. (2 Thessalonians 3:6-15) Buying books and tapes. (1 Samuel 9:6-10) And then there are those checks in the mail with a simple, *"Thank you for an encouraging word."* (Philippians 4:16)

Make no mistake, money is always welcomed. This is how we make our living, after all. But I am not skilled enough as a writer or a speaker to convey to you how important it is that you get it. So never ever forget it, you are greatly appreciated.

ABOUT THE AUTHOR

Michael E. Evans is an expert at discovering, developing, and maximizing the potential in people. A self-described **M-B-A,** *(Minister, Businessman, Artist)* Michael exercises these gifts to develop leaders and establish churches by helping people **Find, Follow & Finish** *their course.*

Since January 1, 2003, Michael has been sending out a daily e-mail from **The EncourageMINT** to subscribers around the world. He has self-published three books: **Getting Out of Debt & Staying Out** (Out of Print), **One Nation Under Attack...***Understanding the Creation of the Nations*, and **A Dream Lies Dead**.

It is our prayer that this devotional will be a blessing to you and your family for generations to come.

Good Morning Lord!

AN ENCOURAGING PRAYER

Thank you for another day -- filled with life and renewed mercy.
Thank you for providing for my salvation through the death burial and resurrection of your son Jesus. I receive your precious gift of life by faith today.
I repent of any sin in my life and accept your forgiveness and cleansing now.

Thank you that I am healthy.
Regardless of how I feel at the moment, I believe that Jesus was wounded for my transgressions and bruised for my iniquities. The chastisement of my peace was upon him and with his stripes -- I am healed.
Thank you for filling me with the Holy Ghost.
The same Holy Spirit that raised Jesus from the dead, dwells in me and quickens my mortal body, making it alive and vibrant.

Thank you for calling and choosing me. I know I did not choose you, but you chose me and ordained me that I should go and bring forth fruit and that my fruit should remain.
I will go Lord! I will go and preach the gospel. I will go and teach all nations, baptizing them in the name of the Father, the Son, and the Holy Ghost. I will go in love: love for you and love for my neighbor.

Thank you for setting me into a family of believers.
Thank you for your gifts of apostles, prophets, evangelists, pastors, and teachers.
Thank you for filling me with peculiar gifts and talents, as well.
Thank you that all my gifts are making room for me.

Thank you for meeting my needs according to your riches in glory by Christ Jesus.
I will be a faithful steward. I will be obedient to your heavenly vision. I will work as unto the Lord. I will pay my tithes, honor my just debts, give offerings, care for my family, and help those that are in need.

All these things I commit myself to as you aid, undergird, assist and strengthen me. Don't make me so poor I am tempted to steal. Don't make me so rich that I forget you. Give me things that are convenient for me.

I will not worry fret or fear. For you have not given me the spirit of fear but of power, love and a sound mind. I will trust you Lord and cast my cares on you. And I will wait on you Lord.

I will occupy until you come.
I will worship you and praise you and look for you glorious appearing.